The enthusiasms of the Centerbrook partners
are embodied in the design work they create.

THE MASTER ARCHITECT SERIES IV

The Enthusiasms of Centerbrook

Written by William H. Grover, Jefferson B. Riley, Mark Simon,
Chad Floyd, and James C. Childress
Edited by John Morris Dixon

First published in Australia in 2001 by
The Images Publishing Group Pty Ltd
ACN 059 734 431
6 Bastow Place, Mulgrave, Victoria, 3170
Telephone (61 3) 9561 5544 Facsimile (61 3) 9561 4860

National Library of Australia Cataloguing-in-Publication Data

The Enthusiasms of Centerbrook.

ISBN 1 86470 047 5

1. Architecture, Modern—20th century.
I. Dixon, John Morris, 1933–. II. Grover, William H.
(Series: Master architect series IV.)

720

Written by William H. Grover, Jefferson B. Riley, Mark Simon, Chad Floyd,
and James C. Childress
Edited by John Morris Dixon
and Renée Otmar, Otmar Miller Consultancy Pty Ltd
Cover design by Cummings & Good, Chester, Connecticut
Page design by The Graphic Image Studio Pty Ltd,
Mulgrave, Australia
Printed in Hong Kong

Contents

Acknowledgments

We would like to acknowledge and extend our sincere gratitude to the following people and organizations who have supplied us with materials for this book, have given us inspiration over the years, and shared our enthusiasms through thick and thin:

William Turnbull, Jr. and Donlyn Lyndon of MLTW; former partners Robert Harper and Glenn Arbonies; landscape architect, mentor, and friend Lester Collins; Jim and Liz Watson, Jack Richards, Morgan Browne, Art Brings, Bruce Stillman, and Susan Cooper (now at the Trudeau Institute) all of the Cold Spring Harbor Laboratory; John Lahey, Pat Healy, and Joe Rubertone all of Quinnipiac University; Gordon DeWitt, Marge Boley, Reed Bergwell, Jack Wilson, and George Hathorn all of Dartmouth College; Larry Schilling, George Kraus, John Alvarez, Art Dimock, Tom Gutteridge, and Jack Veiga all of the University of Connecticut; Brad Hastings and Mike Ballard of the Pomfret School; collaborators Hugh Brown, Henry Shriver, Aubrey Brock, Mariette Himes Gomez, and VisionFactory; delineators John Blood and Nick Deaver; clients who took daring chances Syoko Aki, Tim Boyd, Shelley Kaplan, Jim Brickman, Jim and Donna Reid (twice), Susan and Bob Buchanan, Jim and Martha Shattuck, David and Amy Jaffe, and John and Lyssa Miller; John Jacobsen of White Oak Design; The National Endowment for the Arts for its support of Chad Floyd's research of American settings for celebration; The William Wirt Winchester Traveling Fellowship from Yale University; Melinda Blauvelt; set designer Eugene Lee; authors, scholars, and observers of how people inhabit cities William H. Whyte, Kevin Lynch, Spiro Kostof, Ray Gindroz, and Michael Dennis; architects Cab Childress and Robert Venturi; chroniclers and critics of architecture James Marston Fitch, Vincent Scully, Jr., and Robert Campbell; The Moving Target Jazz Band and The Essex Corinthian Jazz Band; the early and courageous supporters of our television adventures Horace Huffman in Dayton, Bern Ewert in Roanoke, and Dick Bornholdt in Watkins Glen; scholar of sacred spaces, music, and art John Wesley Cook; Bob Burt and the United Church of Christ Fellowship of Architects; artist Arthur Thrall; our supportive parents, spouses, siblings, and children; our many wonderful and enthusiastic clients; especially all of the dedicated and talented associates and employees, both past and present, of Centerbrook; our skilled and professional consultants and engineers; our marvelous photographers.

This book would not have been possible without the able and dedicated assistance of our Manager of Public Relations, Genie Devine nor without the critical counsel of our editor and friend, John Morris Dixon. We would also like to recognize Sharon Dougherty, Leslie Henebry, Nelle Jennings, and Lora Olivieri for their valuable contributions.

Our special gratitude is extended to our long-term clients of many years, Cold Spring Harbor Laboratory, Quinnipiac College (now University), and Dartmouth College.

Last, we would like to express our deepest appreciation to our teacher, mentor, and former partner, the late Charles W. Moore, FAIA, who showed us how to design our enthusiasms into buildings.

"We act as though comfort and luxury were the chief requirements of life, when all that we need to make us happy is something to be enthusiastic about."

Albert Einstein

Twentieth-century culture places high value on new scientific and technological discoveries such as those of Einstein's. This is especially true in the world of architecture where buildings often are judged by the degree to which they sweep aside the past. But Einstein himself was not so doctrinaire. He took special pleasure in the infinite variety of human enthusiasms and considered their expression a high priority.

At Centerbrook, we are encouraged by this insight from a father of our scientific era. For us, progress is more complex than just an expression of newness. It embraces all tenses available to the imagination—past, present, and future. We see a complex cultural universe that calls for a multiplicity of viewpoints.

This book is not a manifesto or an instruction book. Rather, it describes enthusiams that have shaped our buildings. While among us we share many attitudes, our individual viewpoints sometimes diverge. Yet, always we have let our enthusiasms animate and guide our work.

The book is dedicated to our clients, who have stimulated our best efforts, and to the many talented people with whom we have collaborated in the past and with whom we will venture into the future in our enduring mill building on the Falls River in Centerbrook, Connecticut.

Bill
Jeff
Mark
Chad
Jim

Introduction

By John Morris Dixon, FAIA

How many firms would write a book about their enthusiasms?

Most architects have enthusiasms, of course, that drew them into the field in the first place, then sustained them through years of demanding education and practice. But they are usually hesitant to talk about their enthusiasms. Instead, the education and experience of architects tend to focus their attention on deficiencies. Criticism and self-criticism are endemic in a profession that calls its encounters with school faculty 'crits'. In an architect's early years of practice, there is much pressure to design defensively, as though to fend off criticism. The result is a lot of cautious design; a lot of architecture that follows established formulas.

The enthusiasms of the Centerbrook partners are embodied in the design work they create—not only the specific enthusiasms you will find so well explained in this book, but also a belief in taking chances, in pursuing your enthusiasms even if they lead to unfamiliar design territory. The avowed enthusiasms of these architects are wide, encompassing Fourth of July parades, theatrical set design, pick-up games, and improvisational jazz. Clearly, they share a great enthusiasm for people. Too many architects consider people mainly as obstacles to their self-fulfilment. At Centerbrook, the experience of people in the buildings the firm designs is the foremost consideration. Rather than discussing proportions, refinement of details, or perhaps fragmentation as a metaphor for our present condition, they talk about how a sitting area overlooks a busy pedestrian path. And they are clearly skillful at communicating their enthusiasms to their clients and to the communities with which they often exchange ideas.

The Centerbrook partners aspire not just to house activities in their buildings, but also to nurture and enhance these activities through the physical settings they design. And they pursue these aspirations with equal enthusiasm, whether the job is small or large.

There is a profile for the jobs they want—and get. Their commissions usually involve alterations to an existing situation; catalytic interventions that improve an area much larger than the specific job. Much of their work is on campuses, piecing together an environment with a sense of place out of initially unpromising elements. Much other work involves generating new activity zones in urban areas that have become moribund. In several cases, they have had long-term, repeated commissions from the same client, resulting in the gradual transformation of a complex (as at the Pfizer plant), or the generation of a distinct environment where little had existed before (such as at the Quinnipiac College and Cold Spring Harbor campuses).

Behind the Centerbrook partners' enthusiasms are keen and continuous observations of architectural settings and the life that goes on within them. And, as this book clearly demonstrates, they excel in the interpretation and reporting of their observations, as well as in applying what they learn in the design of the firm's projects.

In all of this, the partners follow a tradition traceable back to the late Charles Moore, their teacher and mentor, who was a partner when the firm was established (as Moore Grover Harper) back in 1975. One of Moore's salient ideas was something of a revelation for me in 1973 when, speaking at a *Progressive Architecture* Awards dinner, he advocated 'vulnerability' as a virtue architects should possess. He was referring to the same kind of openness to stimuli from a variety of sources—inside and outside the field of architecture—that the Centerbrook architects exhibit. Most architects were then striving to become as invulnerable as possible in order to preserve their egos, their principles, and their design individuality within a world that constantly challenged them. Along with architect Robert Venturi (with his collaborators Denise Scott Brown and Steve Izenour) and the urbanist Jane Jacobs, Moore opened many minds to a more encompassing architecture that could respond to popular needs.

The architects who joined Moore in the several offices he helped to found shared his willingness to accept and to learn from a variety of stimuli, and so did the next generation of architects who are now included among the partners at Centerbrook. They are people with broad interests and active involvement in the world beyond architecture. Like Moore, they have developed ways to gather input from the community so that their works can knowingly embody the public will. And they are able to express their interests and recommendations in engaging, persuasive prose.

All that thoughtful observation, all that attention to user input, all that sensitive organization of the firm to foster creativity would mean little if Centerbrook did not produce architecture of exceptional quality. The firm's work over the past 25 years has earned them many awards, much praise, and the attention of thousands of respectful colleagues. When the American Institute of Architects bestowed its one-per-year Firm Award on Centerbrook in 1998 (admission: I was on the seven-member jury), they were cited for consistently producing "human-scale spaces filled with delight".

The firm, now numbering some 85 people, is housed within a group of old brick-and-frame mill buildings, picturesquely spread along the Falls River in the bucolic village of Centerbrook, Connecticut. The firm is structured as a constellation with five equal partners: Bill Grover, Jeff Riley, Mark Simon, Chad Floyd, and Jim Childress. This is not a traditional partnership, with members assigned areas of responsibility (design, production of contract documents, business development, and so on), but more like a group practice, with partners running their own jobs from beginning to end, sharing staff and quarters. Though responsibility for any one job is only rarely shared, everyone at Centerbrook works in unpartitioned spaces, where discussion of design takes place spontaneously. All of the partners benefit from the influence of their peers and the firm's whole staff.

Although the firm's work is inspired by humanistic concerns, computer technology has been playing an increasing role in this practice. Centerbrook's early and thorough adoption of computer systems reflects partner Bill Grover's life-long interest in electronic devices. In this book, he describes how he generated ornament on an oscilloscope long before computer graphics was born. The firm's use of computers does not, however, show up in complex and hitherto unattainable building geometrics. The building industry Centerbrook deals with is not ready for that, anyway. Instead, computers in this firm facilitate exploration of many more design options than could previously be explored and allow for the sharing of these explorations with clients and community groups. A limitless variety of renderings and walk-through videos assure a full understanding by everyone involved in a project, and e-mail communications transferred onto compact discs record for posterity the resolution of every construction challenge. Centerbrook's ex-urban location in no way discourages their adoption of the latest technology.

Centerbrook's work has already been published in two previous monographs on the firm. The partners feel that it is now time to share the ideas behind their designs with other architects and the interested public. They have conceived this book as a collection of essays of varying length by every partner, illustrated in part with examples from the wide world that inspire them and in part with their own works that embody the lessons they have learned.

I have thoroughly enjoyed being a sounding board for the partners' ideas and helping them (in the role of referee and—yes—critic) as they fine-tuned their essays for this engaging and provocative book. Like the Centerbrook partners, I believe that inspiration need not be limited; it can include villages in India along with mansions of Parisian nobility, low-tech construction techniques along with high-tech. I am happy, also, to see a couple of contemporary works by other architects cited as inspirations, because they are two of my favorite, too-little-recognized projects: Roche Dinkeloo's Creative Arts Center at Wesleyan University and Rafael Moneo's Davis Museum and Cultural Center at Wellesley College. Like the many other examples cited in this book, these projects produce no obvious echoes in Centerbrook's work, but add to the firm's collective understanding of architectural possibilities.

We hope you will browse through the pages of this book, reading what appeals as you go. The contents are meant to be accessible as well as thought provoking. Do not treat it as assigned reading. Enjoy what you want to explore today, and return to the book tomorrow, when other topics may capture your interest.

Centerbrook's partners gather beside the Falls River dam that channels
water beneath their building. They are (from left) James C. Childress,
William H. Grover, Jefferson B. Riley, Chad Floyd, and Mark Simon.

Our Enthusiasms

Chapter 1 The American Way

Bill Grover

There is something unique about the American way of coming up with architectural ideas. It stems, probably, from the way in which the country itself came together. Our ancestors were rolling stones, dissatisfied people looking for something to be enthusiastic about; looking for new ways to do new things; looking to get away from old things; looking for ways to collaborate while still retaining individual freedom. American art, music, dance, technology, business, and architecture all show the influence of this restlessness. Early architecture focused on the basics: keeping warm and dry using available materials. In our variety of climates, buildings naturally assumed different, efficient shapes. A flat roof, for example, requires more materials than a pitched roof if it is to support a heavy snow load. Our industrial and agricultural buildings assume their shape from their function.

1

2

1 The basic grain storage building is a symbol of the power of American agriculture.

2 Home, sweet home.

3&4 The design for the Dekalb Plant Genetics Laboratory was influenced by Midwestern Barns.

3

4

While accommodating the basic requirements of architecture (to keep the weather out), we have social reasons to refine or elaborate on the rudimentary shapes. Many builders of buildings want to show off their individuality and want to demonstrate that they are unique, while others do not give a damn—they just want to keep warm, dry, and profitable. Others take the opportunity to make a political or polemical statement, and still others just want to be good neighbors and fit comfortably into their community. The buildings people build and occupy make, for better or worse, a statement about who they are. Everyone who builds, renovates, or occupies a building has a dream of what it will be. The architect becomes the interpreter of what the owner or occupant wants to say, and adds his or her education and experience to the endeavor. Interpreting the dreams of our clients and exceeding their expectations is the great challenge and the great pleasure of architecture.

5

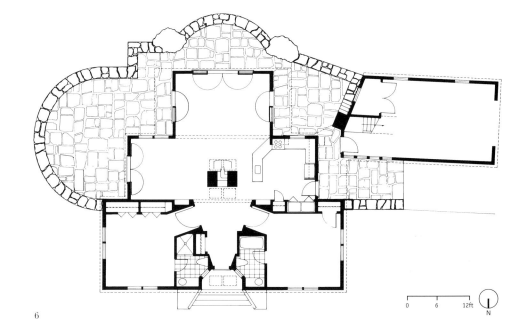

5&7 The Baldwin House is a small, functional cottage with aspirations of grandeur.

6 The Baldwin House floor plan exhibits American functionality and efficient use of space along with European symmetry.

6

0   6   12ft

N

8

8&9   The House in Killingworth is a collection of gable-roofed "barns" and connectors in a variety of common agricultural colors.

10   "Waney-edged" boards for the roof sheathing extend the barn-like character into the living-room.

9

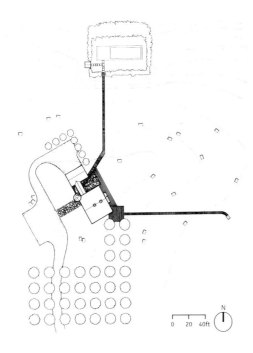

11

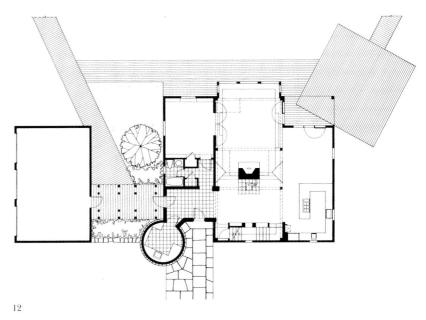

12

13

14

11 Site plan
12 First-floor plan
13 Second-floor plan
14 Plan of loft
15&16 Boardwalks across the fields connect the house to the corn-crib gazebo and swimming pool, with miniature barn for a pool house.
17 The Miller House is comprised of three simple agricultural forms that sit with zen-like serenity in a hay field.

15

16

17

20 Enthusiasms of Centerbrook

20

18   A highly transparent, black iron railing maintains the open view from the deck with Williamsburg grace.

19   The additions to the House in Southern Connecticut, a 1970s contemporary house, uses New England agricultural and residential forms to make it "homelike".

20   Contrasting colors help to reduce the apparent size of grouped multiple buildings.

21&22   The idea of this house is to give the impression of a tent camped out on a hill overlooking the river and a bit of treehouse, too.

23   The Rowe House has a distinct "entry" side and "view" side which are expressed differently in both color and form. The view side is the color of tree trunks so that the house nearly "vanishes" when viewed from the river below.

24   A grand entry to a tiny house.

21

22

23

Chapter 2 Mongrels

Mark Simon

It is often said that mongrels are sturdier than pure-bred dogs; they are calmer and less likely to get sick. That may be pure "foofaraw", but it appeals to me. I also like the exploration of mixing two breeds and finding something new. It seems very American.

America is a melting pot of peoples. Our culture comes from a stirring of the pot. Some of America's greatest art forms—jazz, modern dance, rock 'n roll, abstract expressionism, and Broadway musicals—are blends of the various cultures that ended up here. Our eclectic culture has also shaped our architecture.

Some reject or feel shame in the mix; to them, greatness lies in purity, especially in that of European pedigree. While a singular vision offers an apparent *gravitas*, I revel in our mongrel heritage. I think that is where our strength lies; it is what gives us our special energy. We are the best of alloys.

Cooking offers another analogy for this mixing. We can blend things together, as in a smooth soup, so that the ingredients are not visibly distinct but together make up a unique flavor. Or, we can make stews with separate morsels, each with its own flavor to enjoy in concert with the others. The morsels are best when they counterbalance one another, sweet against sour, firm against soft. Either mix can be a delight.

The singular vision requires refinement. We Americans are not as likely to refine as we are to invent or experiment. The only ideal we seem to evolve on a continual basis is that of our democracy, which demands a constant shifting in order to stay in balance.

Occasionally, our invention overwhelms us with newness. This leaves us craving for some tradition to hold on to, to assure us that we are not lost. At the same time, we won't give up our desire to continue tasting something new. Hence, in America we find new and old mixed, rather than separate and juxtaposed, as is often seen abroad.

1

1   In our Pond House, bracketed Victorian
     cottages, roofed with colonial ship-makers'
     arches, have modern rhythms in their
     fenestration.
2–4 The Chemistry Building at the University of
     Connecticut in Storrs recalls local mill
     buildings while simultaneously drawing cues
     from its campus neighbors, both Collegiate
     Gothic and Modern in style.

2

3

4

5

5   Simple Greek Revival pavilions and chimneys at the Ross-Lacy House separate into discrete modern elements within a complex modern composition.

6   Floor plan of the Ross-Lacy House.

7   At the Guyott House, Victorian arches imitating the French Gothic-Revival carve into the solid boxes of the American Shingle style.

Opposite:
  The Pond House uses the simple materials of New England—tongue-and-groove painted boards and slate-fronted fireplaces. When cocked at varying angles, the fireplaces speak with a Modernist grammar.

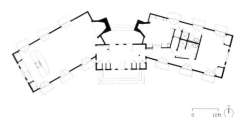

6

7

26 Enthusiasms of Centerbrook

9 The Crowell Studio is a shoreline summer cottage elevating itself into a lighthouse.

10 At the Island House, Japanese castles wed the American Shingle style with Frank Lloyd Wright presiding to sire a new breed.

11 In the Pond House, modern, basket-woven wood trim plays against Gothic arches and colored plaster walls that are reminiscent of the Italian Veneto.

12 The get-away pavilion on the Marsh Estate has a faux truss—blending traditional materials with modern abstract gesture.

9

10

11

12

13

13 The House near Washington, DC—never seen before (or since): Tudor Japanese.

14 The great camp of the Marsh Estate uses the imagery of a Boy Scout jamboree in its tied ropes.

15 Dekalb Plant Genetics Corporation's modern agricultural research lab impersonates a barn.

16 Greek Revival dormers dance on the roof of an industrial shed at the East Lyme Community Center.

14

15

16

17&18 and Opposite:
    Nauticus, the National Maritime Center, is a
    21st-century aircraft carrier on one side
    (opposite), a futuristic, deep-sea oil derrick on
    another (17), and a sea monster on a third (18).

17

18

Chapter 3 Jazz and Bumper Cars

Bill Grover

Jazz

Of all the creative arts, architecture is probably the slowest. From the time a design is begun until the building is occupied typically takes several years or longer. Improvisational jazz, on the other hand, is probably the fastest. The jazz musician, thinking within some general guidelines of tones and rhythms, must decide on a pattern of notes to play, then play them, analyze the outcome, and, based on that analysis, decide what notes to play next—all the while listening to fellow musicians who are doing the same thing and are reacting to each other in order to make a coherent, or at least interesting, piece of collaborative work.

In comparison, architecture is like playing several melodies and harmonies simultaneously over a period of years. After the building dedication, the architect analyzes the final result and adjusts the plans for the next building to take into account what has been learned from the last. But, because of the long time between concept and completion, it is difficult to base the design for a new building on the results of the last one. It is interesting to consider that the ideas for a recently completed building were initiated years before. Then, too, one does not really know how well a building was designed until it has been in use for some

1

time. The best buildings are those that have been in constant use for many years, renovated a few times, and yet are still inspiring to their occupants.

2

Bumper Cars

There is, however, an interesting parallel between jazz and architecture. In a typical improvisational jazz piece, there is collaboration between several musicians. They usually play a first chorus in ensemble to establish the concept of the melody line and basic chord structure. Each musician then plays an improvised chorus or two based on the underlying structure, and finally the ensemble plays a final chorus to consolidate and conclude the piece. As each musician plays, he or she listens to the others, and the resulting improvisation is thereby influenced. At Centerbrook, we are influenced by what others are doing. We feel free to take a "riff" or two from someone else's melody and to elaborate upon it. The mixture of collaboration, improvisation, suggestion, and encouragement has been inspirational.

One of the especially nice things about practicing architecture with a team is the delightful and unexpected result that a collision of disparate ideas can bring.

Driving alone in a bumper car is not much fun. Crashing into others is far more exciting. Several people sitting around a table with paper and pencils can come up with better and more interesting notions than each working alone—provided that the individuals keep an open mind and are willing to set their personal agendas aside for a while, letting the ideas build on one another. This method of design is the most fun and, ultimately, the most satisfying, though it takes careful criticism and filtering to be able to maintain a clear idea. Our late partner, Charles W. Moore, was especially good at this way of working. A great designer, he taught us how to seek ideas from everyone, how to separate good ideas from bad, and then how to fit them together joyously and coherently.

3

4

Chapter 4 Discovery vs. Pursuit

Jeff Riley

Some people live their lives in earnest pursuit of happiness. Others, with no less purpose in mind, simply discover joy wherever they can find it.

When it comes to the making of architecture, I find it interesting to apply these two divergent approaches and useful to distinguish between them. The *pursuit of happiness* approach assumes that happiness can be defined and that a prescribed plan of action can be followed in order to achieve it. It is intentionally selective and, therefore, an exclusive approach. The *discovery of joy* approach is, alternatively, serendipitous and largely unplanned. It is intentionally collective and, therefore, an inclusive approach. Of these two approaches, my enthusiasm lies with the latter when applied to architectural life.

Architects in "pursuit of happiness" commit to an established architectural style (or to one they have developed on their own) and, with admirable devotion, strive to perfect it, excluding those things that might interfere with their aesthetic vision. They hope for, in the end, a "pure-bred" body of work. This approach has, indeed, given the world some of its most distinguished-looking buildings. Nonetheless, its preoccupation with a single direction has often impoverished architecture by robbing it of the complexity that so characterizes America's increasingly diverse culture and that, one could argue, deserves expression now more than ever.

In contrast, architects who consider the process of design to be one of "discovering joy" embrace the complexity of our culture. They value its variety and open themselves to its many surprises. They are willing to consider anything that suits the people for whom they are designing or the situation at hand. They look for the possibilities in things, even when those things appear at first to be unpromising. They are more likely to favor a "mongrel", as Mark Simon would describe it, that is adorable and loved by the neighbors than a "pure-bred" that might win first prize from the judges at the show.

"Discovery of joy" buildings sometimes eschew a discernible style altogether in the interest of responding fully to their circumstances. They might be called "non-buildings". They are buildings that do not appear, at first sight, to be buildings as we normally think of them. Instead, they appear to be a garden wall or a gateway or a fishing pier, or they may disappear altogether below earth mounds or merge into the woods. The architects of these buildings have placed appropriateness above their own expressive urges. In each instance, the architect has been able to abandon his or her identity and become a medium through which the spirit of the place is revealed. T.S. Eliot advanced this idea by arguing that an artist's progress is "a continual extinction of personality". As the world becomes more crowded with buildings of unbridled, individual expressiveness, those that have been fashioned by the joys of a place and that offer suitable fits have their appeal.

1&2   Reid House II on Cape Cod is less like a traditional summer cottage on the shore and more like a ship with promenade decks that gain views of the ocean and surrounding harbors.

1

While the "pursuit of happiness" approach is focused on style and all its virtues, there is, nonetheless, a growing fatigue amongst both architects and lay people with the fashionable, stylistic changes in architecture today, even while they acknowledge "style" for having had value in the past. Style has galvanized architects' attention for millennia and has served at least three significant purposes. First, it has been used to convey a specific ideology. The Greek style, for instance, conveyed notions of the human ideal and democracy. The Gothic style conveyed the concept of sacred place. The Prairie style represented authentic American virtues and aspirations. The International style argued for the equality of all humankind, and so on.

Second, architectural style has been used to establish certain proportions, scale, ornament, detail, materials, and even color, with which the architect could confidently achieve some level of beauty with consistency.

Last, style was a means by which the architect's expressive ego was sublimated into the culture. Individual expression took the form of incremental refinements of a style. Style was not fashion to be outdone by next year's model, but rather an attempt to express a culture that was not likely to change overnight.

3

4

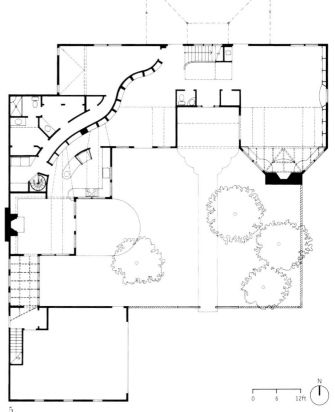

5

3–5　Situated on a busy boulevard in Cleveland Heights, Ohio, Reid House I appears at first from the street to be a simple fence with an arched gate. Appropriately, the fence shields the house from the noise and dangers of automobile traffic. Only after entering through the gate do you discover the oasis and house that lie within.

6–8　The Wriston Art Center in Appleton, Wisconsin takes on the form of a low-brick "garden wall" in order to mediate between a five-story Modernist limestone library to the north and a one-story student center to the south which was built in 1949. Hidden beyond the "wall" are the crystalline walls of the Center and an amphitheater.

6

7

8

But those who are attracted to the "discovery of joy" approach to architecture side with the belief that architectural style no longer serves these purposes very well. Architectural style began to lose its former stature with the advent of post-modernism, a movement born in the early 1960s with MLTW's (Moore, Lyndon, Turnbull, Whitaker) Sea Ranch Condominium in California and later advanced by Robert Venturi's enormously successful book, *Complexity and Contradiction in Architecture* [New York: Museum of Modern Art, 1966]. That beginning held great promise. MLTW's project opened the door (and many architects' eyes) to an architecture based on a sense of place. Its focus was on how humans might inhabit that place in meaningful ways. Venturi's book was an erudite and provocative polemic on the ways in which architecture could enrich our lives by being more inclusive. It deserved the serious consideration it got.

In 1962, Charles W. Moore (the "M" of MLTW, and our teacher, mentor, and partner) wrote, "A useful distinction might be made between the *general* solution and the *specific*. The general solution, whether curvily sculptural or puritanically cubed, is the diagram of an independent idea, conceived in isolation; the specific solution starts with a place, makes it habitable, and enhances the qualities of the specific place by making it responsive to the needs of the people who use it (in all those ways we find it hard to communicate)." He goes on to say that "... our troubles start from too much that is general and too little that is specific, too much that is expression and too little that is response, too much that is invention and too little that is discovery."

Today, well over a third of a century later, we continue to struggle with those same excesses, perhaps to an even greater degree. Although post-modernism's initial focus was on the act of habitation and away from stylistic movements, it nevertheless became known as the "style-crazy" episode of American architecture. Instead of leading to investigations of architectural *performance*, it led straight to an *aesthetic* reaction to what many saw as modernism's stylistic "dehumanization". Regrettably, we ended up with too much that many people felt was frivolous and

9

self-indulgent. The results were severely criticized by some as mere "façadism". Architectural style had become mere fashion, and soon the dangers of being merely new were upon us.

Today, the ability of architectural style to convey an ideology in America is all but gone. Our society, as a whole, is too diverse ethnically and culturally to have the necessary common ground. Often, talk about style and ideology occurs only among intellectuals. But most people cannot inhabit buildings that require deliberate intellection in order to be appreciated. We are not built that way. As far back as 1933, architect and journalist James Marston Fitch argued: "We cannot be happy in a house that appeals only to the brain—we have not that much brain. We are too fecund, loving the rounded corner and the devious way; we are still more human than not ..." ["These Houses We Live In—An Anonymous Lament" by James Marston Fitch, *Architecture*, volume 68, October 1933]. Two-thirds of a century later, it seems that, for most people, a meaningful and enduring architecture appeals to their senses, emotions, and instinctual needs more than to their intellect. They respond with enthusiasm to buildings that have managed to capture the joys of their particular lives.

Thomas Jefferson's Great Lawn at the University of Virginia is a good example of how our emotional response to a work of architecture is both independent from and more enduring than our intellectual response to its "style". Jefferson's use of architectural style was intended to convey a precise ideology. He rejected the French Rococo style because it symbolized to him a corrupt monarchy. He chose instead the classical style, convinced that "... Greek democracy and Roman republicanism offered the correct parameters for constructing a new society in America". Jefferson's campus is in fact a veritable encyclopedia of the styles of classical antiquity because he thought they would serve as "specimens for architectural lectures" and would help prepare the students for a role of leadership. Architectural style carried weight back then.

10

For most of today's society, however, Jefferson's Great Lawn carries none of that ideological gravitas, and yet, after a century and a half, it remains the center of a great modern university. The reason for its enduring viability lies in the way in which Jefferson's campus *performs* for people. Its landmarks, paths, edges, and ambiences help to orient its inhabitants and to create for them a memorable mental image of the place. It is a dramatic experience to walk through the campus. Spaces contract and expand. There is a sense of threshold, that is, of passing from the outside world into this one. It has textures, colors, aromas, sounds, materials, inflections, scale, and proportions that please the senses and create a memorable ambience. It has sociability and provides a setting for public gatherings and community celebrations, its two rows of dormitory pavilions forming a well-sized and pleasingly proportioned enclave, and

its magnificent Rotunda providing the backdrop and focal point for all sorts of pageantry (see Chad Floyd's chapter on "Celebration"). In short, the Great Lawn enhances the act of human habitation in basic, instinctual human ways. Indeed, those who feel that the world today suffers from too many overbearing stylistic triumphs might say that the Great Lawn still works because its architectural style does not interfere with its intrinsic ability to perform for people.

There no longer appears to be a compelling argument for a singular architectural style such as Romanesque, neo-Georgian, modern, post-modern, or neo-modern. Instead, we might want to discover the joys of styles from cultures all over the world and to combine a few chosen ones anew into the designs of our single buildings for the American melting pot. To style we might assign the purpose of adding "color" and "flavor", like spices,

rather than a meaty, ideological one that aspires to the conveyance of great meaning. What becomes important is the sense that we are each a part of the whole life of the world. The meaning will come from how these stylistic elements are put together with the other parts of the building, and how, in the end, the architecture nourishes people.

There is a danger here that many architects and critics worry about. Architecture critic Robert Campbell, for one, warns that "… if we all go on speaking each other's architectural language and imitating each other's culture, the result will be worldwide architectural entropy. The built world will decline from difference into sameness." He goes on to suggest that the answer is to "… discover and cultivate a kind of design that will retain its cultural language without copycatting the past."

11

This is an argument for the "discovery of joy" approach to architecture. It argues for a genuineness in architecture that comes from capturing the essence of a place, an essence that can only be achieved through empathy. That, in turn, requires, as T.S. Eliot understood so well, the loss of "self" that, too often, interferes with the act of empathizing. It requires that the architect be ready and willing to *discover the joys* of that place. "Regionalism" doesn't have to be a recitative response to an established local style, but rather an innovative response to climate, contour, vegetation, and available materials and technology. "Contextualism" needs no longer to be a matter of dexterous stylistic fit with neighboring buildings, but rather a fit of scale, materials, color, placement, orientation, traffic patterns, and, importantly, deference when respect is merited. "Style" becomes a less serious choice for each architect and owner. They can, in ways that are appropriate to the circumstances of their specific situation, select from historic styles or more current ones; or they might cleverly combine some, or invent their own, or ignore style altogether and make a "non-building".

It may be feared that the "discovery of joy" approach is disinterested in the way a building looks, so long as it looks interesting. But, in fact, it argues for the dominant visual concern of architecture to be beauty, not a specific style, to be more of the emotions than of the intellect. We should rediscover the generics of beauty. Beauty can be a deceptively simple thing, although it is not always simple to achieve.

We do not depend upon new architecture to provide us with beauty. Beauty is eternal. It does not depend upon the choice of or fidelity to a style (otherwise, why would styles come and go?). Rather, it comes out of the establishment of a certain relationship in the building's inanimate parts (their shape, size, number, arrangement, and inflection), the aesthetic purpose of which is to imbue them with the qualities of life. And, in this definition, beauty is not a question of taste or obedience to a set of rules set by a tenured few, but is instead something that can be sensed by all people of all cultures and at all times because it is born of human sensibilities.

The process of discovering the joys of a particular place, client, or community connects us with the growing complexity of America's culture. It is an antidote for our society's growing and often alarming "expressive individualism" that undermines our sense of community. It nonetheless allows for America's mythic "utilitarian individualism" which extols self-reliance and achievement and which was the quality that helped build this country (see Bill Grover's chapters on "The American Way" and "Not Reading the Instruction Book"). The "discovery of joy" approach to an architectural life is the most promising path for the individual toward our destiny as a cosmopolitan society.

> *"Modernity is the transitory, the fugitive, the contingent, one-half of art of which the other half is the eternal and the immutable."*
>
> Baudelaire

13

13   At our Shapiro Admissions Center at Brandeis University, the entry is enlivened by natural shapes which give the building an immutable beauty not based on any particular architectural modernity or style.

14–16   The Lender School of Business Center at Quinnipiac College serves as the main gateway into the campus and appears appropriately and remarkably as no more than that, when seen from the north (16). It is not until you come through the domed rotunda that you realize you have walked through a building and into the campus.

14

15

16

17

18

19

17 The Colby College Student Center was situated strategically on the main footpath connecting the two halves of the campus. Appropriately, it was designed as a bridge over the path.

18 The dome of the Lender School of Business Center reverently echoes its backdrop, the majestic Sleeping Giant Mountain.

19–21 As viewed from a rural road, the House in the Hudson Valley in upstate New York is a simple arrangement of Federal style farmhouse and connected barns. A typical New England procession takes you through a garden gate and welcomes you into an herb garden. Only then does the full realization of the playful family retreat unfold.

20

21

Chapter 5 **Stagecraft**

Chad Floyd

Countless hours in undergraduate theater productions have left me with an enduring enthusiasm for the scene designer's art.

Yale Dramat designers regarded themselves as seminal framers of stage action. With canvas and paint they created a magical atmosphere that set the tone for productions and nurtured in the audience what Elizabethan dramatist Ben Jonson (1572–1631) called a "willing suspension of disbelief".

The source of that magic was nothing more than a few stage directions and a careful reading of the script. From little else, student designers at Yale, such as the brilliant John Jacobsen, who later founded White Oak Design, fashioned complex environments of doorways, platforms, windows, steps, and furniture. These elements gave directors the playing fields they needed in order to assign movements to actors through a process called "blocking the play".

Plays were blocked well before the start of rehearsals. In order to do so, the director had to have in hand the designer's scenic layout, which he studied while annotating the script with movements actors should make, down to the smallest detail. Directions were as simple as turning downstage right to exit a door (motivation: to enter a drawing room) or turning upstage left to climb a rampart (motivation: to obtain a vantage point for viewing a battle).

Interplay between the stage layout and characters' motivations for engaging it had to be plausible and—amazingly, I thought—had to have been anticipated by the scene designer long before the director blocked the play.

The style, color, and shape of stage backdrops were what provided the production with atmosphere. In modern life, the word atmosphere has an imprecise and, in architectural circles, even a pejorative meaning, but in the world of theater gets respect. Atmosphere is what sets the tone for a play and makes stage action plausible. In theater, nothing could be more important.

It was remarkable how independently our college scene designers operated. Leland Starnes, the Dramat's professional director, left them pretty much to their own devices. I wondered how our designers were able to create settings for stage action from little more than words on a page. Eventually, I learned the secret. They methodically charted overlay upon overlay of action until the potential movements of each character—and hence the sum total of demands on the stage set—were understood. It was not until then that the designer actually began to design the stage set.

1 The set of "Breaking Point", designed by John Jacobsen at Yale in 1964, with Chad Floyd at right, about to break a phonograph record in a fit of pique.
2 Poster with Chad Floyd, in costume at Yale, 1964: "Breaking Point", by William Fairchild.

1

AMERICAN PREMIERE

Six Men Isolated Beneath
the Arctic Snows
⅋⅋
Feb. 25, 26, 27
at 8:30 pm
February 27
Matinee at 2:30 pm

BREAKING POINT
BY
WILLIAM FAIRCHILD

Reservations:
University Theatre Box Office
222 York Street
Telephone 865-4300
Mailing Address: 902A Yale Station
⅋⅋
A
Yale Dramatic Association
Presentation

PRIOR TO BROADWAY

2

This realization convinced me that the scene designer's art is not about ego, as it so often is with so many painters, sculptors, and architects, but quite the opposite; it is about empathy, or subordination of ego. A scene designer's inspiration is the script alone, and he is true to it.

At Yale, pride was taken in designs of startling versatility. I remember the great Eugene Lee, then a student at the Drama School and soon to rise to Broadway fame, who, chameleon-like, followed up a madcap production of DeGhelderode's "Death of Doctor Faust" with a starkly geometric set for "The Country Wife", a Restoration comedy. How the man could follow the one with so different another was beyond me.

But my outlook on artistic accomplishment at the time had been shaped by art history courses at Yale. In the art history classroom, it was the practice of professors, like archaeologists describing the process of evolution, to trace the incremental development of an artist's congealing style as evidence of his or her artistic worthiness.

This did not prepare me for Gene Lee. His designs—sharp, startling, laser-like realizations of scripts—were totally unpredictable. His only signature was ingenuity and excellence. Gene's work was never about himself, and it did not try to be universal. It was responsive to the needs of each show, with spectacular results. Watching Gene convinced me that the design of stage scenery is a different kind of art from the paintings, sculpture, and architecture I had been learning about in the classroom.

This ego-suppressed approach has seemed to me a very good way to design architecture, also. For all the profession's focus on objectness, buildings ultimately are about commodity for habitation, and, like scripts, the conditions of habitation vary. With the many "scripts" that have come Centerbrook's way, it has been a very considerable pleasure to try to respond to each one as being unique.

This may account for the diversity of Centerbrook's work. I hope it helps to explain why our projects are not much about the personal predilections of the designer and a lot about the making of a place.

3   The Broadway production of "Ragtime" was the ultimate realization of Lee's concept.
4   In this design drawing for "Ragtime" (1998), Tony Award scene designer Eugene Lee uses mixed media to illustrate how he plans to incorporate large-scale projections into a fixed armature.

3

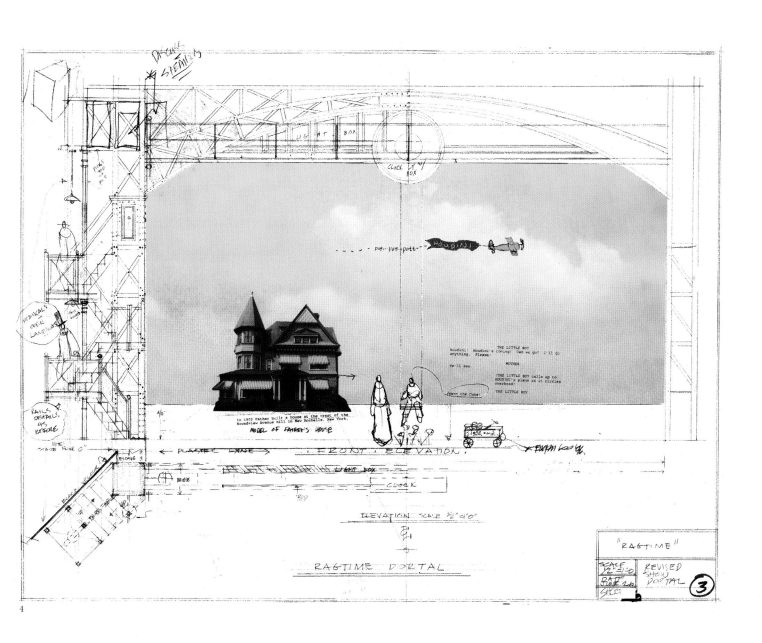

MODEL OF FATHER'S HOUSE

In 1902 Father built a house at the crest of the Broadview Avenue hill in New Rochelle, New York.

FRONT ELEVATION

ELEVATION SCALE ½"=1'0"

RAGTIME PORTAL

"RAGTIME"

REVISED SHOW PORTAL

③

5

6

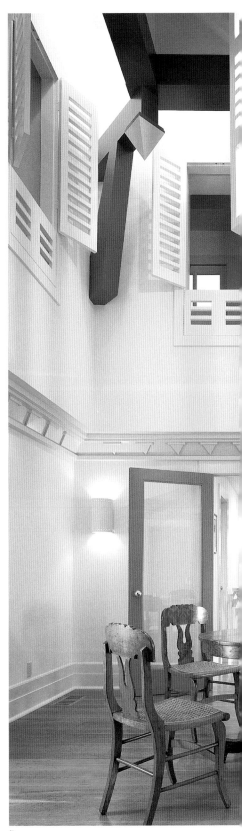

7

5   Farmers' stalls in downtown Roanoke, Virginia, provide water, electricity, and shade while creating an environment in which farmers "perform" and the public "reciprocates".

6   Central Lakes College in Brainerd, Minnesota, is a prairie building with an atmosphere of color and shape inspired by graphic traditions of the nearby Chippewa Nation.

7   Inside the House in the Country, a tall foyer admits layers of light from a high cupola while communicating a character inspired by Bavarian villages and churches fondly recalled by the German-scholar half of the client couple.

8   The House in the Country uses ideas about rural barnyards to create a country living atmosphere.

8

9

9&10   At the Hood Museum of Art at Dartmouth
College, this stair keys into Jean Cocteau's
hand-held sconces in "Beauty and the Beast".

11   The Main Gate facility at Pfizer's Groton,
Connecticut pharmaceutical plant draws on
the site's maritime history as a World War I
and World War II shipyard.

12   This renovation of a two-car garage on Cape
Cod strives for the quintessential beach-
cottage feeling.

13   Samuel's Clothing Store has the feel of a
fashion runway. Changing booths are
mirrored boxes on wheels and lighting is from
a pipe grid. The idea is to invite patrons to act
out fashion-model fantasies, while buying
clothes with abandon.

10

11

12

13

14

15

16

14 The previous Tuck School's dining hall was the
    starting point for this common room, which
    provides students with an appropriate venue to
    practice social graces.

15 This modest shed at the South Gate of the Pfizer
    plant in Groton is what it looks like—an
    employees' entrance shack. Making a building
    convey its purpose is not necessarily easy.

16 Students at the Tuck School of Business
    Administration at Dartmouth College dine in a
    room meant to accustom them to futures as
    business titans.

17 The twisted geometries of this House on the
    Connecticut Seashore are generated by a variety
    of views, wedding it to the site.

18 The house uses louvers to recall seashore places
    in the Caribbean and Asia.

17

18

19

20

21

22

19 The wood finishes of this living room in the House in the Country make it a good recital room for the pianist client. The ecclesiastical colors are intended to inspire a reverent ear.

20 This tiny fishing pavilion sets up a memorable identity for a site in New York's Finger Lakes, making connections to places in the Adirondacks.

21 Like a garden folly, this pool pavilion hints at pleasurable pastimes for visitors to House in Greenwich, Connecticut.

22 Clusters of electronic workstations under bright metal umbrellas create an air of sociability for the Babbidge Library at the University of Connecticut, Storrs.

23 These gleaming new laboratory modules at the Jones Laboratory of Neurobiology, Cold Spring Harbor Laboratory create a dramatic, high-tech setting for state-of-the-art science.

24 This Library in New York City is a setting redolent with scholarship.

23

24

25 Moving through mysterious, reef-like layers on a gently inclined moving sidewalk gives visitors to Nauticus, the National Maritime Center, a feeling of being underwater.

26 At Quinnipiac College, a growing institution with no previous law tradition, this new Law School projects an air of jurisprudence.

Opposite:
A courtyard for special events at the Norton Museum of Art in West Palm Beach puts people on center stage in a South Florida setting.

25

26

Chapter 6 Pick-up Games

Jim Childress

I have never been very serious about team sports, perhaps because I was never very good at any sport involving a ball, but mostly because I have found many team sports, ironically, to be more about strong individuals and less about playing together. That is the reason I am drawn to pick-up games, where the group is always more important than any individual, and where it is essential to discover people's strengths and the ways in which they can complement the others on your team.

Although architecture is a team effort, it is often practiced by strong individuals who take the lead, direct people, and provide the conviction needed to see a bold design through to completion. One definition of architecture is the ability to say, "I can" in the face of everyone else's saying, "you can't". Certainly "signature" buildings need a strong singular design direction in order to succeed. However interesting the "star quarterback" might be, I am enthusiastic about the potency of designing collaboratively. Architecture can excel when practiced like a pick-up game.

Businesses are becoming less dictatorial and more team-oriented. This collaborative model is attractive in part because it gives everyone the opportunity to contribute, and it boosts morale. But it also recognizes that a single idea or direction is limited. Alan Greenspan understands that economics is a product of many ideologies. It requires analysis and "bending with the wind"—stiffening when appropriate, relaxing when necessary. Architecture may not be a fluid profession, like economics, but the process of designing can be.

A one-person office is lonely. The camaraderie of others, the challenge of their critiques, the volleying of their different ideas, and working with non-architects offers great pleasure in its messy vitality. It is not always easy. Egos can be bruised, partners can quickly become too dictatorial, and the staff can feel under-appreciated. The creative potential is diminished when one person emerges as the star quarterback or domineering coach. It is best when members of the team operate as though they were musicians in a band. No one person stands out. Instead, harmony and dynamics combine to make something that is transcendentally beautiful.

1

2

3

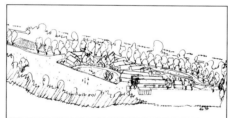

4

5

1 Many people—clients, students, colleagues, builders, and citizens—add layers of interest to the design of buildings with which they are allowed to get involved.

2–5 By sketching alternative concepts, it is possible to explore imagery with clients. In designing a new campus for Hamden Hall Country Day School in Hamden, Connecticut, we considered four different images for the new campus with the help of a committee of 30 people.

6–15 At the University of Colorado's Health Sciences Campus Center alternative plans and images were considered by those who work in the building. They usually have the best instinct about which plan works well and what is the most appropriate character.

Collaboration works best when everyone has an equal role, yet offers different strengths. The collaboration has to take place around a big table, either in reality or figuratively. It doesn't work if one person goes off to a private room to dream up a design for a particular detail and then returns to tack it on without discussion.

Dale Chihuly, the renowned glass artist, once talked about his large glass chandelier installations in Europe and Mexico. He could have designed them by himself and hired artisans to fabricate them. Instead, he chose to design with a team of the world's best glassblowers. All of the marvellous creative invention took place collaboratively. First, the team explored the spaces where the pieces would be installed. Then it dreamt up ideas and built mock-ups. Chihuly gave the impression that the collaboration was as important as the final product. Participants discovered things they would not have on their own. Indeed, the chandeliers have a creative energy that appears to exceed the abilities of any single artist working alone.

It is fairly universal in architectural thinking that good design requires the designers to truly understand the place and the people for whom they are building. One of the best methods of gaining this understanding is to see the project through the eyes of the people who know it best. For a house, these are the homeowners themselves; for a college they are the professors who have taught there for years and the facilities people who know how to take care of the place; for a church they are members of the congregation. Often, design is hard to talk about, and the people who are asked to get involved have difficulty in articulating their feelings. It is the architect's role to ease their minds and help them to join in with the give and take of design.

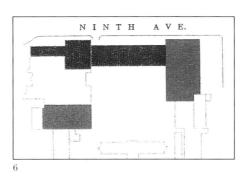
6

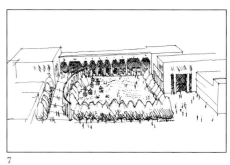
7

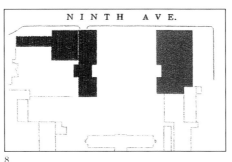
8

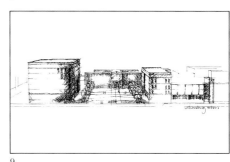
9

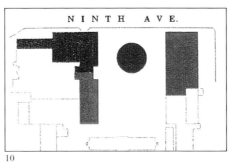
10

11

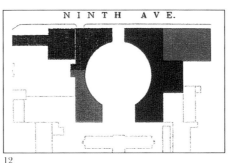
12

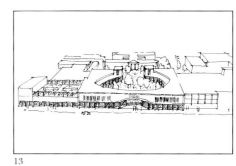
13

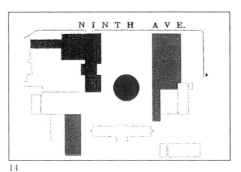
14

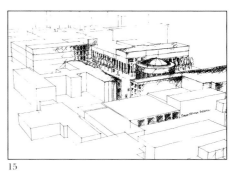
15

We have learned many successful strategies for facilitating people's participation in the design process. We are always trying to discover more. We have developed the use of 'games' to provide people with a way in which to communicate patterns of movement, functional relationships, and major and minor concerns. We have conducted 'beauty contests' to explore issues of character and appearance—on both the exterior and the interior. We use slides of other places and sketches or models to explore different possibilities.

Architectural students have recoiled in horror at the idea that an architect would ask a non-architect what a design should look like. However, if your goal is to really understand a place, the insights of non-architects are invaluable. Clients never ask us to "make it look just like that". People are more complex and interesting than that. Their input is an attempt to communicate a spirit or a character that is meaningful to them. The architect has plenty left to do to capture, in the final design, the essence of what the users are conveying.

People are drawn to buildings that are at once familiar and inspiring. If a design has some familiarity, people are able to understand it and communicate how they feel about it. If a design is totally out of their experience, there is no point of reference by which to talk about it, and it becomes meaningless to them. Conversely, if a design is all too familiar, it feels like no one cared about it, and it is considered "common". The challenge is always to strike the proper balance between familiarity and inspiration.

The most successful buildings and places are those that have this balance. These buildings have a patina, that is, a layer of time that does not reveal who designed them or when. New England villages and campuses, such as Brown University and Berkeley, have developed over the years with the input of many people. Moore Ruble Yudell's recent additions to the Powell Library at the University of California, Los Angeles and our changes to the Pfizer Pharmaceutical plant have many layers of ideas and a dimension of human complexity that cannot be achieved by one individual.

These are the ultimate benefits and satisfactions of playing with a group of people. By letting outside forces influence the design process, we make our buildings more meaningful and more likely to communicate to more people and for longer periods of time.

16 Some architectural elements were deleted and others added to the Powell Library at the University of California, Los Angeles by Moore Ruble Yudell. The resulting layers of images provide interest.

17&18 In designing the Hamden Hall Country Day School, we used cartoons and found that even subtle differences in details conveyed different meanings to our clients. One image was too residential, one was too barn-like, but a certain combination of images was just right (18).

16

Bashful

Grumpy

Happy

Doc

Dopey

Sneezy

Sleepy

17

18

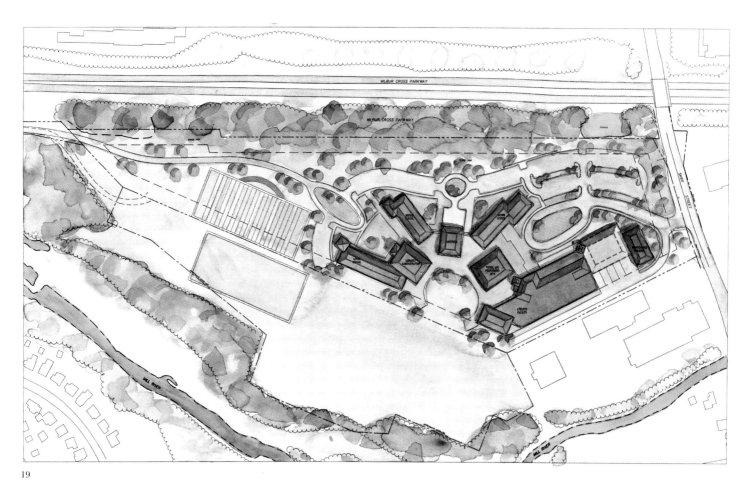

19

20

21

19 The final plan and imagery of Hamden Hall Country Day School was the result of input from the entire school community.

20 The character of the campus was developed by exploring alternative images, seeking one that would be appropriate for a private day school that must compete with other prep schools.

21 Small interventions, such as gooseneck lights and steel railings, add a layer of imagery—in this case nautical—to Pfizer's ever-evolving waterfront complex.

22 At the Pfizer Pharmaceutical Plant in Groton, Connecticut, a new entry gate builds on the existing industrial image of the campus. The layering of new and old enhances the whole plant, even those parts left untouched.

22

23

24

25

23&24 The additions and renovations to the original Power House, now called the Luke Building, at Cold Spring Harbor Laboratory in New York required a collaboration of sorts among buildings, both new and old.

25 We added new layers to the existing Power House that blur the distinctions between who did what and when.

26 The forms of the new buildings are familiar to the existing ones, while subtle twists contribute a new layer.

26

Chapter 7 Sculpture

Mark Simon

I am the son of a sculptor. Though art was the family business, I wanted to work with others, not alone in a studio, and became an architect. Even so, sculpture is still with me.

My father carved figures out of logs, following the twists and turns of the wood. Of course, his pieces told stories as human figures, but the wood also spoke. It showed how it grew and struggled with nature. Its color darkened with age in ways that stain could never match, becoming richer with time. Newness has its gleam, but patina glows. Materials have a life of their own that deserves attention.

Sculpture teaches other lessons for architecture.

In order to best appreciate sculpture, the observer must see it transform—by moving the eyes across it, or walking around it, or watching it through the day's changing light. This requires time. The sculpture should invite the observer to do this—to spend time with the piece. So it is with architecture. Architecture can invite people to walk around or (better yet) through it for observation, stopping occasionally to appreciate forms, spaces, light, color, or details. Time and architecture work together.

Sculpting the human body teaches that what is beautiful is not as perfect or symmetrical as we might imagine. This is easily seen when holding a vertical mirror at right angles to one's face, along the center of the nose, and then reversing the mirror. We have two different half-faces! So too, our sides are different, inside and out (we have a right brain and left brain; our heart is to the left; we are right-handed or left-handed). Our minds desire to make things more symmetrical and perfect than they appear, and, sometimes when designing, we would like to make our buildings more perfect than they should be, or can be. Imperfection can be beautiful.

Sculpture often draws from natural forms, especially bodies. Bodies move. Sculpture tries to capture movement in a variety of ways—by moving the observer around, through moving parts, like a Calder mobile, but most often through gesture. Gesture is a frozen motion. For some reason it seems to work when the motion is apparent, and yet stabile. There is a tension in this resolution of motion and stability that offers pleasure. It is seen in great classical Greek sculpture and in the best of abstract sculpture. It is also seen in great architecture. Called "dynamic balance" by some, "occult balance" by others, it can animate buildings, making them like creatures about to move or in the act of moving. This can attract attention, or can tell stories; it can announce a use, or promote itself. It can bring a place to life.

1

1 As with sculpture, materials play an important role in the experience of a building. Every room in the Marsh Estate Lodge is finished differently, highlighting materials. In this stairway, birch bark is applied to the walls with copper brads, its reverse side exposed. All will darken gently with age.

Opposite:
Our small house, Simon-Bellamy I, huffed and puffed itself upwards with a mock grandeur.

3 *Rebellious Slave*, Louvre, Paris
  Michelangelo twisted his figures in order to
  dramatize their gestures and "stories."
4 The pavilions at the Ross-Lacy House bend around
  the entry. The grand windows at its ends drip like
  swags, to suggest ornament and to add a sense of
  weight in this spare frame house.

3

4

6

5 My father, Sidney Simon, played with the wood grain in his carved work.

6 Even small gestures in my father's sculpture could convey profound meaning. In this self-portrait, his hands are imprinted on my brother's body, and his ears are missing to declare his deafness.

7&8 The fence defining the entry courtyard at the McKim House has pickets that start orthogonal at the left end, but become "drunken" and random as they proceed. The pickets echo manic stickwork elsewhere around the house as well as the tipsy windows across the court and spinning rooms inside.

9 First-floor plan

5

7

8

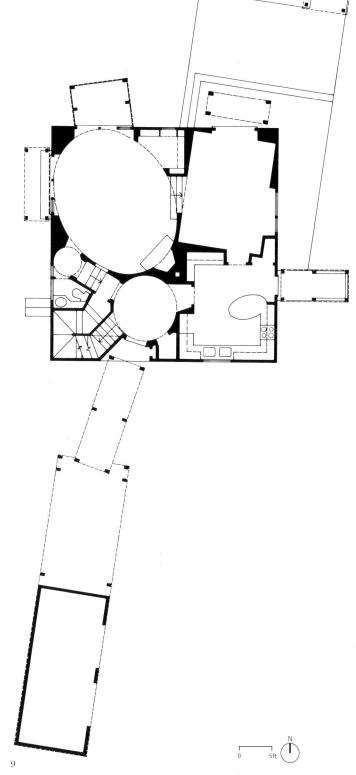

9

0   5ft

N

10 Balusters walk down the stairs.
11 The Marsh Estate flaps its roofs like a big bird's wings.
12 "Drunken" railings assist the visitor to the entry.

10

11

13

14

15

16

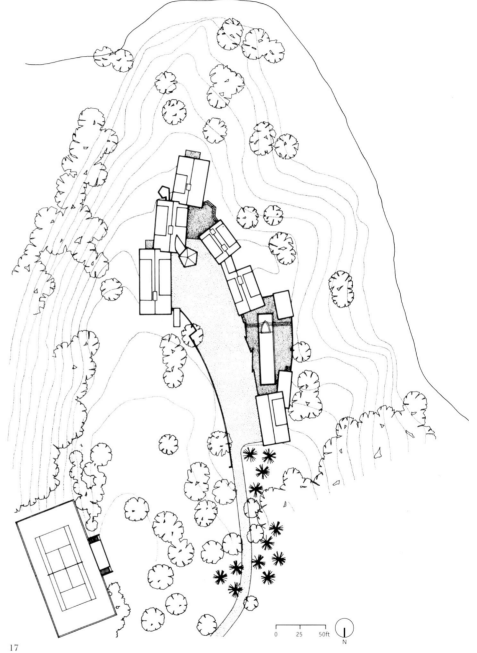

13 The Pond House's roofs and chimneys billow in the wind.
14 Ceilings billow upstairs in the Pond House.
15 Windows dance like waves.
16 The entry tower steps into the courtyard.
17 The pavilions curl around the entry court.

17

18

19

20

18   Animated brackets lift the porch roofs at the Pond House.
19   The Pond House's library spins with brackets and shelves.
20   Our egret is catching a dripping fish above the Guyott pool.
21   The entry arches of the Guyott House bound up their steps.

21

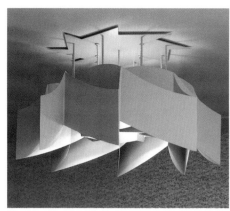

22

22&23 The dining room chandelier of the Guyott House spins like a water eddy, while the brackets of the great room drip like seaweed.

24 The Long View entrance canopy marches out of the building to greet visitors.

25 The two center pavilions at Long View give way to enfold the entry courtyard; at the same time they bow out to the west to gain spectacular hilltop views.

26 Long View's bridal balcony leans over the entry hall as it tosses a welcome to guests.

23

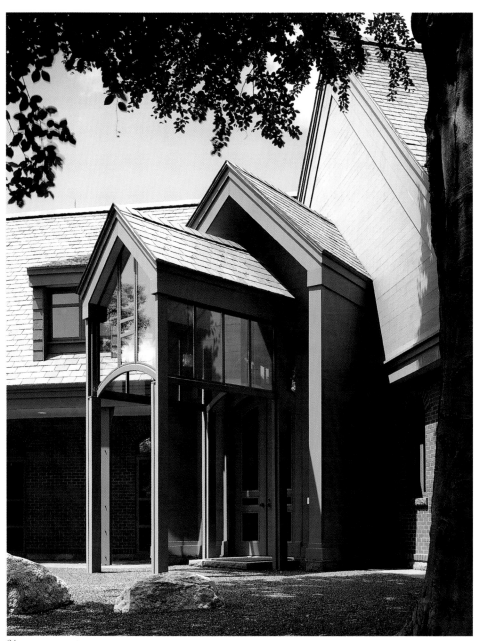

24

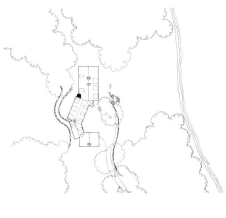

25

26

27

27 The Eisenstein roof spreads out with brackets
    that look like umbrella struts.

28 Curved pavilions at the University of
    Connecticut's new Chemistry Building arc as
    though they are magnetic fields.

29 A bay window over the front entry of the
    University of Connecticut Chemistry Building
    leans out in a bow of greeting.

30 Curved balconies and walls form a fantastical,
    billowing space around Robert Cumming's bas-
    relief mural, as inspiration to scientists at the
    University of Connecticut Chemistry Building.

28

29

30

Chapter 8 Bringing Things to Life

Jeff Riley

It has always seemed to me that much of what it takes to make a building beautiful depends upon the architect's ability to imbue inanimate objects with the qualities of life. I am enthusiastic, therefore, about bringing things to life.

Although literal images impart the qualities of life to a building, beauty is more striking in the subtle abstraction of life forms.

1

2

3

4

1&2　This doorway near the Spanish steps in Rome, Italy, may appear to be humorous at first, but it is both specific and literal and does not allow much latitude for imagination. Alternatively, a light well at our Wriston Art Center abstracts recognizable life forms—in this case a face— and thereby allows for the joys of discovery and mental play. It is the emotional, unconscious connections to life forms that we interpret as beautiful.

3&4　Rhythmic patterns connect us to the measured movements of waves on the water, gusts of wind, ranges of mountains, and the slow spinning of the Earth itself. Inside Quinnipiac College School of Law Center, skylight rafters track the movement of the sun and recreate the dappled light of a forest. A gentle curve repeated at the top edge of each carrel divider brings the space into the sensation of natural things.

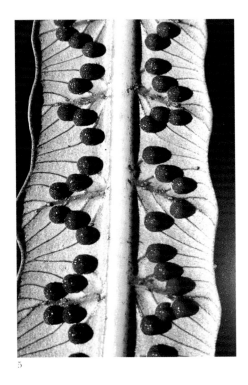

5

5&6 Ordered rhythms and patterns are found in all
forms of life. When imparted to the arrangement of windows and columns at the School of
Law Center at Quinnipiac College, these
rhythms animate the building.

7 Inflection, or the break in a pattern, as shown
in these stone steps in Kyoto, Japan, is also a
basic part of nature. Like the transition in a
piece of music from a major key to a minor key
and back again, inflection combines concord-
ance with discordance, and reflects the
reassuring order that underlies nature's
apparent disorder.

8&9 The slight angle or inflection given to one of
the modules at our Jones Laboratory of
Neurobiology at Cold Spring Harbor
Laboratory gives life to the invading metal
objects that occupy the wood-paneled interior
of this century-old building.

6

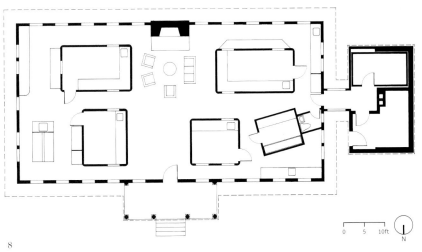

7

8

9

10&11 Occult balance—that is, a symmetry that is not easily apprehended because it is based on the balance of unequal pieces and spacings, rather than of more obvious equal ones—is the way in which much of life takes shape. The Ryoanji Temple Garden in Kyoto, Japan, distills this principle. At our Grace Auditorium at Cold Spring Harbor Laboratory, dormer windows are placed in occult balance. The building leaves the realm of the machine-made and becomes something full of life.

12&13 The Riley House I comes to life by being symmetrical in the parts where a calming effect is desired, such as at the front door, but asymmetrical and in occult balance elsewhere.

10

11

12

13

14–18 Curves can imbue inanimate objects with qualities of life. In nature, nothing has or moves in a straight line (14). Brackets at the Riley House II (15) have the appearance of muscular flex or floral bloom, as do the brackets at the Quinnipiac College Ledges Residence Hall towers (18). The "bow house" at the Reid House II on Cape Cod (17) has the beauty of life forms found in shells, waves, wind-blown shapes, and flowers. Curving wood ribs in the ceiling of the Grand Court Room at the Quinnipiac College School of Law Center mimic vines on a trellis (16).

19–21 We also have an empathetic response to the gentle curvature of our own bodies (19). At the café in the Carl Hansen Student Center of Quinnipiac College (21), it is almost irresistible to run your hand along the curving rail. Curves at the Wriston Art Center galleries (20) reflect the curl of a lock of hair, or the nape of a neck, or the shape of an ear.

14

15

16

17

18

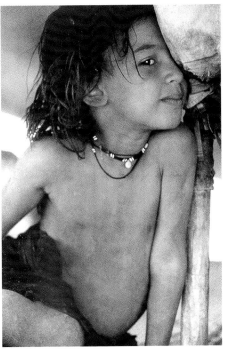

19

20

21

22–24 The anthropomorphic towers at the Quinnipiac College Ledges Residence Hall (22) might also suggest abstracted heads crowned with garlands of flowers or leonine locks of hair (take your pick). Located at the foot of Sleeping Giant Mountain, the towers stand erect like a duo of Etruscan giants themselves. The Reid House I fireplace benches (24) provide natural places to sit linked to our own body shape (23).

25&26 The shape of the human head, where all senses are gathered and processed, has a special connection for us to life forms that we find beautiful. The stair hall window at the Reid House I is a play on Palladian forms, but with more emphasis on the shape of the human form.

22

23

24

25

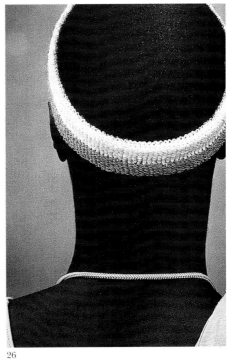

26

27

28

27&28   Whether we are reminded of trees overhead, sheltering caves, or the crown of our own heads, canopies give that same special sense of life to a place. The tower lounges of our Quinnipiac College School of Law Center are capped by a series of domes into which we mentally insert our own head and body. They create, in a sense, a "frame of mind".

29&30   The bilateral symmetry of the human body, although it is not precisely symmetrical (see Mark Simon's chapter on Sculpture), is characteristic of nearly all forms of life. Our House in the Country, likewise, has a bilateral symmetry—a head flanked by shoulders and a torso with arms and legs—to which we have an empathetic, pleasing response.

29

30

Chapter 9 **Celebration** (not the town)

Chad Floyd

While traveling on a fellowship in India in 1973, I became fascinated with the celebrations that periodically transform that country's villages and cities. I returned with enthusiasm for what I saw as a celebration framework underlying the streets and spaces of India's public realm. Bringing streets alive as stage sets for public pageantry seemed a healthy thing, and I wondered whether principles I saw at work in India might be transferable to Main Street, USA.

Like many travelers in India, I was impressed by the adaptability of the country's urban spaces to huge numbers of people. Particularly memorable were the public spaces in the small Hindu village of Pushkar, in the desert state of Radjistan in northwest India.

Pushkar is holy to the god Brahma. Its main street is organized into a path of unfolding mystery for the hundreds of thousands who make the pilgrimage there to honor Brahma on the night of the full moon in October. Pilgrims, in groups representing entire populations of villages, follow a gently rising, very narrow main street. The street organizes the pilgrims' experience into a procession of episodes.

The path yields tantalizing peeks at the sacred Pushkar Lake, which lies a block or so to the left of the main route. Views of the lake are framed by tiny side streets (*ghats*) stepping steeply to the water. While being swept along by the crowd's forward motion, pilgrims are startled by glimpses down the *ghats* of crocodiles preserved through the art of taxidermy in cages at gateways to the lake.

Small village squares offer momentary respite. They are occupied by troupes of performers, merchants selling religious icons, and food vendors. Bands of monkeys look down upon the multitude from perches atop buildings and trees. As I changed film under the shade of a tree, one relieved himself on my head, screeching with delight at my consternation.

The pilgrims' ultimate reward lies at the far end of the village. It is the white temple of Brahma, the only one in all India. And beyond the great temple, spread colorfully across a golden desert, is a spectacular fair with tattered circus tents, a midway, and medieval jousting on camelback. The scene offers the same energized juxtaposition of the sacred and the profane that can be found on market days in other cathedral and temple squares around the world.

I wondered whether the rituals of Pushkar had come first, or if they had somehow been shaped by the streets themselves. Both ritual and street appear to respond to some universal human processionary instinct. In the interplay of ritual and street there is a fine balance, and after six or seven centuries, events and spaces in Pushkar have become inexorably bound. A celebration dimension can be said to have evolved—one that lies very close to the surface, coming alive as the Hindu calendar dictates.

Not long after returning from India, I was able to obtain a grant from the National Endowment for the Arts to explore celebration spaces in the United States. What I found surprised me; I discovered that American celebrations are not so different from those in India—an observation that strengthened my impression of universal principles at work. Rather than commemorating religious fervor as in India, however, American festivals are secular affairs intended to draw attention to memorable qualities of a place, such as the Spanish heritage of Santa Barbara, California, or the hard-driving cowboys of Cheyenne, Wyoming.

Eventually, I found three kinds of space underlying American celebrations, and I noticed how they typically come bundled in what amount to special urban districts—what I came to think of as Celebration Zones.

1

2

1　Pilgrims gather on the stone steps of the *ghats*, or
　side streets, in order to partake of the waters of
　Pushkar Lake during the October celebration of
　the Hindu God Brahma.
2　Pilgrims mount the steps of Pushkar's Brahma
　Temple, the Hindu God Brahma's holiest place in
　India.

Parade Streets

American celebrations are mostly about that great, passively viewed pageantry, the parade. In our society, parades succeed by not asking too much of participants or putting them on the spot. The number-one organizing feature of an American Celebration Zone is the Parade Street. This is a theater for easy-going pageantry. At the small end of the scale, a Parade Street may be as simple as Main Street, USA, the only street in town. At the other end, it can be a monumental avenue defining the epicenter of a large city. Qualities like size, shade, lighting, viewing points, and atmosphere all contribute to a Parade Street's success.

The linear nature of a Parade Street reflects its processional nature. It also provides a useful means for linking elements from the other two categories, Talismans and Enclaves.

Talismans

Talismans are landmarks or object buildings. They are key points of identity for communities. Churches, town halls, libraries, or other imposing structures on downtown streets are Talismans. Almost always bilaterally symmetrical and frequently vertically proportioned, Talismans convey the body image of a person standing. They typically are located on Parade Streets, and are used as backdrops for stationary pageantry.

Enclaves

Enclaves are outdoor rooms, large or small, in which active participation occurs. These are the historic town greens, temporary parking lots, and vest-pocket parks that get taken over for hands-on celebration activities. Enclaves often are located along Parade Streets and frequently have Talismans associated with them. Enclaves are places at a celebration where you can buy food, visit crafts fairs, or participate in ethnic dancing.

Celebration Zones

Combining all three elements, Celebration Zones are the spiritual heart of America's communities. They often define the center of downtown. Relationships among elements within a Celebration Zone may be straightforward, as one would expect in a modest town perched astride a single Main Street, or complex, as in a large city such as New Orleans, which contains several Main Streets, each with unique combinations of elements. There can be—and usually are—several Talismans and Enclaves in a Celebration Zone, but typically only one Parade Street.

Over time, I have come to believe that celebration elements may well be universal across cultures. The Yang of the Talisman, male and ultimately iconographic, is balanced by the surrounding spatial Yin of the female Enclave, and the two are linked by the mesentery of the Parade Street. This is as accurate a characterization of what I saw in Pittsburgh as what I saw in Pushkar.

With this Celebration theory to draw upon, Centerbrook has by now introduced Enclaves, Talismans, and Parade Streets into many urban and campus contexts. And we have often tried to equip our Celebration Zones with simple amenities such as power, water, and even switchable streetlights for easy transformation into night-time celebration mode.

The pace of change in American communities is far swifter than the rate at which the ancient village of Pushkar evolved, and the American environment is driven by a vastly more complex dynamic. By introducing the Celebration dimension into American places, Centerbrook hopes to satisfy fundamental human needs that otherwise might be left wanting in our fast-changing and technology-based society.

3   Parades are an easy formula for staging large-scale spectacle, asking little of participants. Floats are moveable fantasies, especially here in Covington, Ohio, in 1976.

4   The 4th of July Parade in Bristol, Rhode Island, is the largest in the country, with a fine Parade Street. Front porches are transformed into shady box seats.

5   Boothbay Harbour's waterfront parking lot is a small Enclave for pageantry during "Windjammer Days".

6   The United States Capitol Building acts as a national Talisman every four years when it is the backdrop for the presidential inauguration.

6

7

8

9

7 Talismans with strong vertical proportions, such as the Santa Barbara City Hall, attract temporary stages. The stages benefit from the character of the Talisman behind.

8 Mardi Gras is enhanced by narrow, 24-foot French Quarter streets and multi-tiered balconies, which make the crowd and huge floats seem even more exciting. With Krewe members throwing coins to spectators, Mardi Gras parades are the most participatory for spectators in the United States—an exception that proves the rule.

9 The Parade Street in Santa Fe benefits from rooftop vantage points on La Fonda Hotel, at right. At the end of the street, the Santa Fe Cathedral is a Talisman from which the parade seems to emanate.

10 A 17th-century drawing of a medieval mystery play in front of an identity-purveying Talisman, an English cathedral.

11 This monumental Parade Street in Cheyenne, Wyoming, is enhanced by its direct relationship to the State Capitol Building Talisman. The building stands tall, is bi-laterally symmetrical, and occupies the end of the street. Architects should not forget the role of symmetry in public buildings.

10

11

12

13

14

12 The Corn Palace in Mitchell, South Dakota, demonstrates the quality of eccentricity that is so essential to Talismans. During the Corn Palace Festival, Main Street is closed, and the building presides over a street Enclave that is used for food and craft activities.

13 Walt Disney had an innate understanding of celebration elements. His "Magic Kingdoms" in Anaheim and Orlando are idealized paradigms of Celebration Zones which combine Parade Streets, Talismans, and Enclaves.

14 A large landing on the steps of City Hall in Springfield, Massachusetts, is a fine platform for outdoor concerts. The large portico behind the building is evocative of the city's identity.

15 During the Santa Fe Fiesta the Santa Fe town square in front of the Palace of Governors is an Enclave that provides plenty of historic atmosphere, along with much-needed shade for food booths.

15

16 The Santa Barbara County Courthouse covers an entire block, with a two-acre park at its center. The park functions as an Enclave for the Santa Barbara Fiesta. One wing of the building facing the park has enough local symmetry to be a stage set of which Busby Berkeley would be proud.

17 Centerbrook's urban design work has benefited from the firm's celebration research. This overlay of downtown Roanoke, Virginia, shows how we identified Parade Streets, Talismans, and Enclaves in a 1979 Master Plan.

18 In order to support festive banners, we obtained easements and installed anchor bolts in the façades of buildings on Roanoke's designated Parade Street.

19 Roanoke's plan has been implemented. This pocket park, a key downtown Enclave, benefits from a new infrastructure of electricity, plumbing, and lighting and becomes a good setting for crafts and food fairs.

16

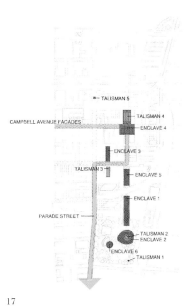

17

18

19

20 Market Square, Roanoke's Enclave, accommodates thousands of people every weekend. A restored 1924 market building is the city's backdrop for pageantry. The building and square have become symbolic of Roanoke.

21 Market Square is used for many other celebration activities, such as alfresco dining.

22 We designed numerous Celebration settings into Roamoke's Elmwood Park.

23 A grassy bowl surrounds an outdoor amphitheater in Elmwood Park.

24 In-ground sleeves were placed along Elmwood Park's walkways to provide a way in which to support umbrellas for shade and fences for displaying art.

20

21

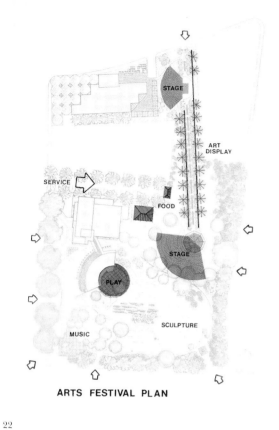

STAGE

ART
DISPLAY

SERVICE

FOOD

STAGE

PLAY

SCULPTURE

MUSIC

ARTS FESTIVAL PLAN

22

23

24

25 For Dayton, Ohio's downtown "Riverlanding"
    we created a river levee that not only
    provides flood control, but also creates an
    amphitheater for concerts.

26 "Riverlanding's" seating overlooks a concrete
    boat that acts as the stage.

27&28 This gorge in Watkins Glen, New York, had
    potential as an Enclave for spectacle. We
    suggested a sound-and-light show,
    "Timespell", to tell the story of Watkins Glen
    from the dawn of time. John Jacobsen of
    White Oak Design produced a spectacular
    show.

25

26

27

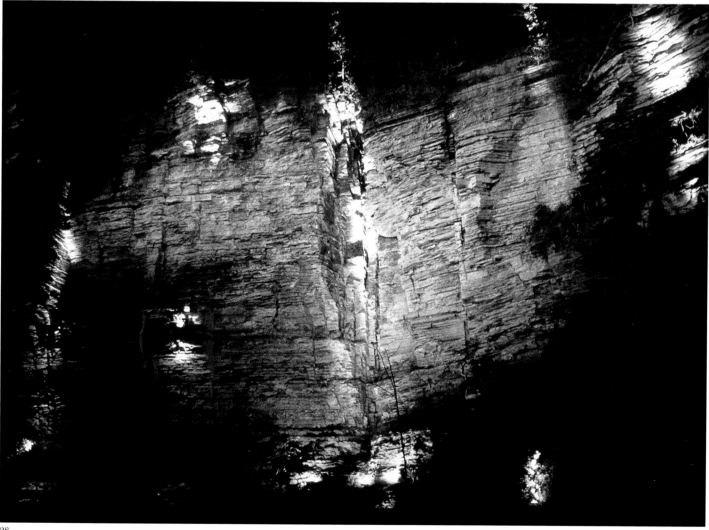

28

Chapter 10 Watercolors and Snapshots

Bill Grover

The camera has made it possible for us to document travels, places, and buildings, easily and quickly. At every interesting tourist venue we see the faces of tourists covered by little black boxes through which they peek at the sights confident that, although they don't have time at that moment to look closely at the scene, they will be able to relive it in their living room at some later time.

Before the advent of photography, watercolors were the way in which travels were documented. Like photos, they are a quick and colorful way to record a moment. But, unlike the camera that stands between the viewer and the scene, they require a close and thoughtful look at the place, imprinting it into the memory. A small watercolor sketch vividly recalls the moment that it was created and the feeling of the place and emotions present at the time. Contrary to popular belief, it does not require major artistic talent either—just a bit of study, practice, and time to observe the scene. It doesn't matter if the sketch is accurate in detail or perspective; a watercolor will capture the moment more passionately and memorably than any snapshot.

1

2

3

4

1 Pitztal Glacier, Austria
2 Santa Maria della Salute, Venice, Italy
3–6 Venice, Italy

5

6

7

7 Tinfou, Morocco
8 Essouaira, Morocco

SCALA RAMPARTS   ESSAOUIRA, MOROCCO   1·13·97   WHG

8

9   Majorelle Garden, Marrakesh, Morocco
Opposite:
    Santa Maria della Salute, Venice, Italy

JARDIN MAJORELLE - MARRAKECH   1·6·97   WHG

9

Chapter 11 Inventions

Bill Grover

My background is one of a collision of multiple enthusiasms, mostly involved in inventing, innovating, and making things. My boyhood heroes were not architects. They included Thomas Edison, Alexander Graham Bell, Charles Kettering (inventor of, among other things, the self-starter for automobiles), industrial designers Raymond Loewy, George Nelson, Norman BelGeddes, Charles and Ray Eames, jazz musicians Chet Baker, Bix Beiderbeck, Paul Desmond, Miles Davis, and many others. I loved to draw and diagram things and to play music. Electricity, radio, electronics, rockets, machines of any kind (especially automobiles and boats), and jazz fascinated me. My enthusiasms have left me with a short attention span; doing the same thing more than once has always caused my mind to wander. Independent discovery was preferable to classroom study. I did try mechanical engineering for several years until I discovered industrial design, a combination of art and engineering where I saw an opportunity to design both the appearance and the mechanical function of things.

I worked as an industrial designer for General Motors for several years, first on a team designing their pavilion and exhibits for the New York World's Fair of 1964-65, and then designing new products and kitchen appliances for GM's Frigidaire Division. It was all fascinating, but I noticed that, for most GM employees, design and making things took a back seat to climbing the corporate ladder. It occurred to me that there might be more opportunity for invention and design in architecture, and that buildings might provide bigger and more interesting design challenges. Unlike automobiles and refrigerators, no two buildings are ever exactly the same, and they offer a wonderful opportunity for invention and innovation.

1

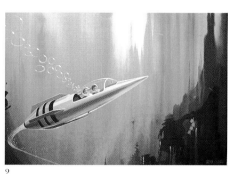

2

3

4

5

1 Radio Boy, 1949
2 Undersea sports car at the General Motors
  pavilion, New York World's Fair, 1964–65
3 Plasma bulldozer at the General Motors pavilion,
  New York World's Fair, 1964–65
4 Prototype for iceboat, 1964
5 Speed-testing the "Ice-bed", 1964
6 Futuristic car, 1960
7 Fold-up airboat, 1961

6

7

Chapter 12 Introverts and Extroverts

Jim Childress

Many of us grow up being shy, and yet wanting to be included in the social activity around us. With growing confidence, we become more comfortable in large crowds of people, enjoying the vitality that groups can offer. Nonetheless, one-on-one conversations with individuals and small groups of people remain important. Most of us have this combination of the extrovert and the introvert within us. I am enthusiastic about the ways in which architecture can create places of intimacy and privacy, while allowing us to simultaneously take part in the larger scene.

A great deal has been written about how to design buildings to accommodate people better. Architects have responded by providing more natural light and ventilation, and by paying attention to good ergonomics. We also need to respond to the ways in which we can foster interaction among people. My partner Jeff Riley has stressed this need for many years. Centerbrook's work at Quinnipiac College in Hamden, Connecticut exemplifies our efforts in encouraging human interaction. Small alcoves off hallways, intimate study rooms with large windows opening onto paths, and classrooms that are configured to have students facing each other are only a few examples of the ways in which we have promoted interaction.

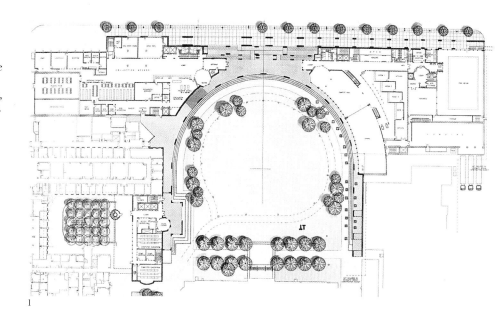

1

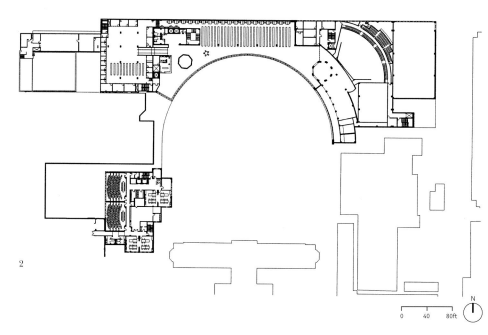

2

1   The new Campus Center for the University of Colorado Health Sciences Center creates opportunities at each entry for chance meetings. The arcaded entry portal directs daily circulation paths around the octagonal rooms designed for hanging out. These rooms also overlook the larger campus common.

2   The library spans the third floor, providing open seating for "extroverts" to overlook the campus green. Smaller, private cubicles, for "introverts", are hidden throughout the stacks overlooking the street.

3&4 The building provides an edge to the campus, scaled to be compatible with the large hospital across the street. The covered arcade provides a protected entry from the parking lot. The ramps and stairs woven in between the piers of the arcade provide private places for people to sit either in the southern sun or in the shade of the arcade. By confining the entry of the campus to this group of portals, we assure a stream of passersby.

3

4

Some of the most successful places for people to interact are not acclaimed works of architecture. One of my favorites is a local Mexican restaurant. It is successful, in part, because the owner has created a place that is full of vitality yet, if so inclined, you can be intimate with your friends. The architecture is full of "stuff" that makes it feel even more active. The seating is arranged in an almost endless variety of nooks and crannies, each connecting to the others.

Places that are built for occasional visits, such as a museum or the latest hip restaurant, benefit from a spectacular "architectural experience" that attracts people by its novelty. In those places, the architect needs to create the entire environment. However, for places that are inhabited on a more or less continual basis, the architecture takes on a different kind of importance. Those places succeed best when the people who live or work there gradually personalize it with their own efforts.

In order to create an active, extroverted space, you need a critical mass of people. This could explain why the more crowded a restaurant or plaza is, the more people want to go to it. In public buildings we strive to create paths that help concentrate centers of activity, and then size them properly so they will feel active and full. The challenge is to create spaces that are expandable to accommodate varying numbers of people without losing that sense of activity when the numbers are low. One way to concentrate people, and to create opportunities for interaction, is to locate something everyone needs in the middle or at the edge of these social spaces. In our own office we deliberately keep only one coffee pot and noticeboard, forcing everyone to convene in one place to use them.

Our own office has proven to be fairly successful in addressing our introverted and extroverted sides. Each person has his or her own private desk. We become territorial about them, reluctant to move because we decorated them with our personal stuff. They are the enclave of our introverted selves. The cubicle dividers are only four feet high, so each of us is part of a larger group in one of three rooms. Small competitions of pride exist between

these rooms to see who can be the cleanest, or who can catch the most fish over a weekend. It fosters, in a subtle way, a sense of being part of a community. At the larger scale, as noted above, by concentrating a few key needs, such as the coffee pot, one becomes part of the overall group at periods throughout the day. Our hope is that one's need for quiet contemplation, active participation, and everything in between is accommodated.

5   At the Lender School of Business Center at
     Quinnipiac College, rooms for team study allow
     for private conversations while maintaining a view
     of passersby in the hallway and lobbies.
Opposite:
     At the Quinnipiac College School of Law Center,
     the central hang-out space in front of the library
     entry has seating in the middle of the crowd
     combined with more intimate seating in balcony
     overlooks.

5

7

7&8 In this house by Trip and Sue Wyeth, two associates in our office, a sinuous wall divides the house into gathering rooms and intimate nooks. By shifting and changing the size of openings between rooms, the architects maintained a sense of privacy in each room while affording a glimpse to adjoining areas. The upper-floor rooms allow peeks into the living area below, giving children the opportunity to spy on their parents' gatherings.

Chapter 13 Escape from Specialization

Bill Grover

Architects just out of school are tempted by the idea of developing a personal "signature style". As young architects trying to figure out how to compete, they naively seek to establish something unique about their work that will cause people to ask them to do more of it. If they are successful at this, there is the possibility that they can find themselves imprisoned by it. Potential clients often want something similar to what we have done before, which makes it easy to fall into an area of specialization and difficult to try something new.

The danger of a "signature style" is that it swings in and out of fashion like a bar-room door. Pablo Picasso drove his dealers crazy. He painted in a number of very different styles during his lifetime, and at each change his dealers thought they had come to the end of their gravy train. Collectors of his art expected more of the same.

Architects can quickly become regarded as specialists, too, either in a particular type of building or by a signature style, thereby excluding themselves from many interesting project types and design explorations. Some firms have been so successful at designing handsome high-rise towers or fire stations that it is unusual for them to be asked to do a single-family house. When architects are interviewed for a project, the first question usually asked is: "How many of this project type have you successfully completed?" If your answer is "This would be my first one", you aren't likely to get the job. One of the biggest architectural challenges is getting a project type that you have never done before.

Architectural practices often begin with a house for a relative. If it is a good house, someone will see it and ask the architect to design another house. The owner of that house may have a small office building that needs renovation. That project may, in turn, result in a commercial renovation. It is important to remember that no project is too small or insignificant to be unworthy of careful design attention. Each is an important step along the path.

Our first project at Cold Spring Harbor Laboratory was a renovation of "Airslie", a house for Jim Watson, who had just become Director of the Laboratory, and his wife Liz. It was followed by a renovation of a small, summer-only laboratory building into a year-round neurobiological laboratory, which won an AIA Honor Award. After that we could say we were "laboratory architects". These project types at Cold Spring Harbor Laboratory were soon followed by a sewage treatment plant, an auditorium, more laboratories, and housing for scientists. We are still busy there, after more than 25 years, with a wide variety of project types we can now show to potential clients as evidence of our specialist expertise.

1   Our first wastewater treatment plant and gazebo at Cold Spring Harbor Laboratory, 1976.
2   "Airslie", the Director's residence at Cold Spring Harbor Laboratory, 1974.
3   Jones Laboratory of Neurobiology (our first lab) at Cold Spring Harbor Laboratory, 1976.

4   Neuroscience Center at Cold Spring Harbor Laboratory, 1991.
5   McClintock Laboratory renovation, Cold Spring Harbor Laboratory, 1993.
6   Grace Auditorium at Cold Spring Harbor Laboratory, 1986.

4

5

6

Inventing a new approach is another way to get a project type that you haven't done before. In Dayton, Ohio, in order to get onto the short list of architects and planners being interviewed for a riverfront planning project, we proposed opening a storefront office in downtown Dayton to get the advice and opinions of the citizens of that city. The idea was so well received by the selection committee that they made it a requirement of all architects being considered for the job. So, again, we had to come up with something that would put us ahead of the game. My partner, Chad Floyd, suggested we should up the ante by proposing to do the design of the project on live television. Chad writes about that enthusiasm elsewhere in this book. That surprising proposal got us the job, and suddenly we had another area of expertise.

7

8

9

A house Jeff Riley designed for a trustee at Quinnipiac College gained us an interview there for the Master Plan of the College and eventually for the design of a dormitory. As we had never done a dorm like this one before, Jeff offered to build a full-size prototype dorm room in our office to demonstrate that his compact and affordable design was workable. Two students brought all of their belongings and spent the weekend living in it and suggesting changes to the plan. That successful dormitory project was followed by many more commissions at Quinnipiac College over the past 20 years, including a health sciences center, a student center, a business school, a law school, a computer center, an athletic center, a library, a maintenance building, and many other new project types. Ongoing relationships of this kind are the cornerstone of our practice and a great source of variety in our work.

11

10

12

7   Our first open-office storefront in Dayton, Ohio, for the Dayton Riverdesign Master Plan, 1976.

8   We developed an urban design for the Riverdesign Study in Dayton, Ohio on live TV, 1976.

9   The Shattuck House, the residence of a Trustee of Quinnipiac College, led to an interview for a Master Plan for the College.

10 A prototype dormitory room, built in Centerbrook's office, tests a new design idea.

11 The new School of Law Center at Quinnipiac College was our first law school.

12 Case study classroom in the new Lender School of Business Center at Quinnipiac College tested a new way of teaching.

Architectural projects can come from entering and winning competitions, although the odds are not very good if it is an open competition. We have, in the past, entered some competitions, but even though we have won a few prizes, none have been built in the way we had hoped, and the effort, while fun and exhilarating at the time, never turned into a real project. Competitions also seem to go against the grain of our design philosophy, which emphasizes extensive and continuous collaboration with our clients from the very beginning of the project, something that doesn't happen in a typical competition format. Still, if you have plenty of time available, and can afford to speculate, competitions are lots of fun. They can result in a building type you have never done before, and you just might win.

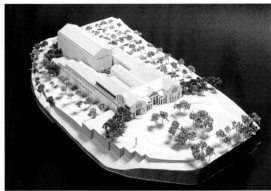

13

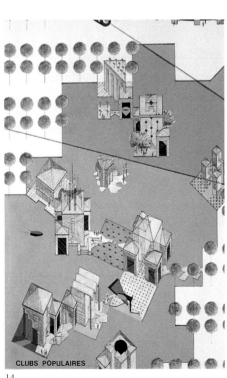

CLUBS POPULAIRES

14

15

16

Connections and friendships are important, too. There is no doubt that a reputation for honesty, cost control, timeliness, flexibility, and professional skill goes a long way toward getting new and interesting projects. A client whose expectations have been exceeded will be the best source of new and interesting work. A prospective client may believe that your reputation for quality work outweighs your lack of experience.

When economic times get bad, as they inevitably do in the business of construction, those architectural firms experienced at a wide variety of project types are the ones more likely to survive and prosper. Specialization is good, as long as you can be a specialist at many things.

We have found that the best way to achieve variety in our designs is to listen carefully to our clients. Listening, without our own preconceived idea of the design, and then paying attention to their needs and dreams as we design with them, almost always results in something new and unexpectedly wonderful.

13 A model of our failed competition entry for the Minnesota History Center in St. Paul, 1986.

14 Centerbrook's Parc de la Villette competition entry (1983) proposed a cluster of island clubhouses. We won third prize.

15 Our competition entry in 1975 for the New Orleans Piazza d'Italia led (eventually) to Charles Moore's commission for the project.

16&17 The Jillson Hill Bridge was our first bridge project. Its character came from a mixture of nearby historic stone thread factories and local legends involving frogs. It was under construction in 1999.

17

Chapter 14 **Surprises**

Bill Grover

The best designs always seem to have an unexpected component that makes them endearing or interesting.

It is okay for architecture to have a sense of humor and to be fun.

1

2

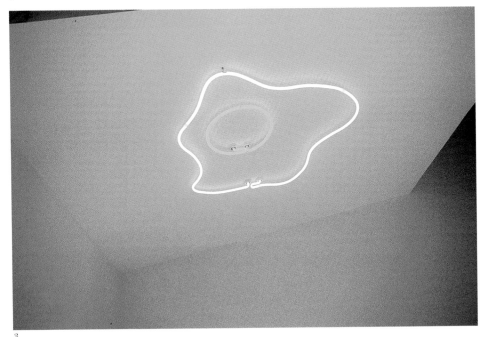

3

1   "Eidolon", a neon-and-fabric ghost, floats above the bed in the Kaplan House.

2   The wind-powered floating fountain on the Miami River, Dayton, Ohio, pumps water up to pivoting barrels which, when full, tip to fill a network of gutters that feed water to a flotilla of flower beds. Wire-mesh, onion domes provide armatures for climbing trumpet vines.

3   The neon "fried egg" lights up the breakfast room of the Koizim House.

4   Mark Simon in the Three Bears Chairs at the East Hampton Library and Community Center.

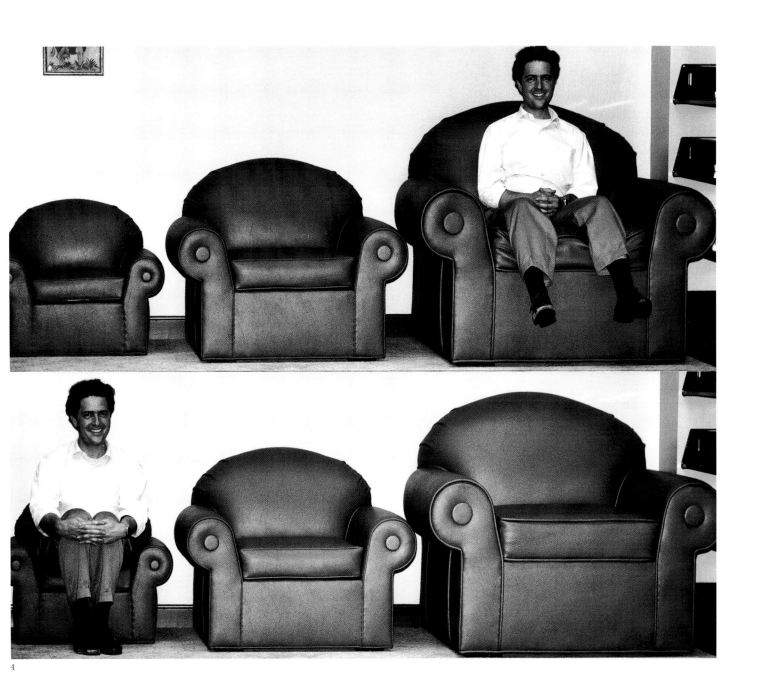

4

Chapter 15 Villages

Jeff Riley

I am enthusiastic about villages as role models for single buildings. A good village responds to the full, complex humanity of its inhabitants, not just to a concern for looks. A good village has a clear organization that helps people to orient themselves and to retain vivid memories of the place. It delights people with its colors, textures, rhythms, patterns, scale, and curiosities. As people walk through a good village, its spaces contract and expand, rise and dip and slip around a corner. There is a clear sense of inside and outside that lets you know you are someplace distinct. A good village has an enjoyable sociability and accommodates community celebration. There is a timelessness to a good village that keeps people interested and makes them feel they are part of a grand continuum.

Fashion, which is the focus of so much pictorial and verbal discourse on architecture, is not the essence of a good village. Indeed, many villages happily accept a patchwork of diverse styles that are sometimes adjusted or modified in order to fit in. This variety adds interest and speaks of the differences among people. The focus in a good village is not the signification of its parts, but rather how its parts come together. The genius of a good village, in many ways, is born of its plan and section and, therefore, lies below the reach of vision. So, in these times of rapid change in architectural fashion, I find myself looking at villages and, with a great deal of satisfaction, applying my observations to the single buildings I am designing.

The observations made here about villages are, for the most part, those of such notable analysts of cities and villages as Kevin Lynch, Spiro Kostof, William H. Whyte, Michael Dennis, Charles Moore, and my partner Chad Floyd, who did such important research into celebration spaces within cities and towns. My interest and effort has been to apply the observations of these authors to designs for single buildings in ways that I hope regain some of architecture's genuineness and meaning for our American culture.

1

2

1&2 The Elliott House in Ligonier, Pennsylvania, arranges an artist's studio, writer's cottage, kitchen wing, entry court, master bedroom tower, and library retreat along a trellised path, much like the buildings along the street of a Swiss village.

Opposite:
At the Riley House I in Guilford, Connecticut, the upstairs bedrooms make small houses within the house. Windows can be opened to smell what's cooking for breakfast, or to talk, or to toss laundry back and forth. It's like a village made up of rooms.

The Way We Shape Our Buildings

We can look to villages for a variety of ways in which to shape our buildings. For instance, villages can either claim a hilltop or merge into it. They can conform in unique ways to the demands of climate. Most interestingly, they can combine different architectural images in one place, yet still have a coherent look.

4

5

6

4–6 Just as the pueblo at Taos, New Mexico (4) mirrors its mountainous surroundings, the Lender School of Business Center at Quinnipiac College (6) was shaped by its setting. In order to maintain the Sleeping Giant Mountain's spell over the campus, the Business Center was kept to one story. The Elliott House in Ligonier, Pennsylvania (5), aligns itself with the edge of a forest fronting a wheat field and, thereby, defers to it.

7&8 Villages are usually shaped by the demands of their climate, such as this Swiss village. It not only spawned pitched roofs with broad overhangs to cope with snow, but also placed buildings and barns close together in order to reduce outdoor travel distances and provide shelter from cold blasts of wind. The shape of a building can also derive from its climate. For example, the Shattuck House, on the Connecticut shore, responds to its New England climate with an active solar heating system housed on the roof of a small, detached summer cottage. The cottage is separated from the main house at an angle, in order to orient its solar collectors to true South and funnel the prevailing southwesterly breezes into the courtyard and through the house during the hot summers. This single house acts in the way that a village does to cope with its climate.

7

8

9&10 Villages show us that many different images can be combined to make a single, cohesive whole. In the Riley House I in the woods of Guilford, Connecticut, images were combined of a cherished log cabin in Northern Maine, beloved Parisian buildings along Rue St Denis, and the clapboard-sided colonial houses for which the town of Guilford is known.

11&12 In the Riley House II, images of the American southwest, (the stucco-and-stone fireplaces), the ancient stone city of Petra, Jordan (the mottled red-stone floor), and the Duomo in Siena, Italy (the horizontally striped columns supporting a pergola) all come together in an harmonious whole.

9

11

12

Organization

We can look to villages to see how our buildings can be well organized for orientation. By the careful ordering of paths, edges, landmarks, centerplaces, districts, and ambiences, a village can be made comprehensible and memorable to the user. These same elements can all be employed to achieve the same clarity in the design of a single building.

13

13&14 Paths help people with orientation by providing a structure for organizing the various parts of a village. It is along paths that all the other elements of a village or city are arranged. At the Lender School of Business Center, the main hallway is a distinctive path. Along the path there are classrooms, lounges, and small team-study rooms arranged like porches along a street. There are also niches, each equipped with a blackboard and a bench, where students exiting classrooms can ask the lingering questions they did not ask during class.

14

15–19 Paths can distinguish a place by encircling it. The Seine River (a type of path) wraps the Île de la Cité in Paris, France (15). At the Striar Jewish Community Center (16&17), the main hallway encircles a grass courtyard clad in Jerusalem stone. The galleries, auditorium, and studios at the Wriston Art Center at Lawrence University (18&19) all encircle an outdoor amphitheater. In both buildings, you can view nearly all the functions inside, leaving no doubt as to where you are.

15

16

17

18

19

20

20&21 While paths encourage movement, edges generally discourage it. Edges can thus give a city or village definition. For instance, the walls of the Kremlin give a strong organization to the city of Moscow. Edges can exclude things, just as the gated fence shields the Reid House I in Cleveland from the noise and dangers of a high-speed boulevard 100 feet away.

22&23 Edges can also enclose a place, create ambience, and serve as useful organizers. The city of Venice is organized around the Piazza San Marco. At the Burns House in Los Angeles, rooms look out onto the pool terrace. The walls that enclose it reflect the morning sun and shield it from views of nearby neighbors.

21

22

23

24

25

26

24–26 Other strong organizers are landmarks. The entry tower at the Quinnipiac College School of Law Center can be seen and approached from either the campus to the south (26), or the driveway and parking area to the north (25).

27–30 Landmarks very often can be the most memorable image we carry away with us of a particular place. Anyone who has been to Florence, Italy will recognize the image at the top left. The master bedroom tower at the Elliott House in Ligonier, Pennsylvania (30) marks the entry court in a memorable way. Landmarks work best when they are unusual, such as the churches in Le Puy, France (28), or the pavilion at our renovation of Wilson Hall at Dartmouth College (29).

27

28

29

30

31

31&32   Centerplaces are another type of landmark.
They occur where paths converge or where
there is a concentration of activities, such as
L'Etoile in Paris. Likewise, the convergence
of three main hallways at the Williams
College Museum of Art is a significant
landmark.

33&34   Districts are also effective organizers. In
villages we often distinguish residential
districts from commercial districts. At the
Percarpio House in Guilford, Connecticut,
the family quarters create a house within a
house, establishing the living and dining
rooms as the public piazzas.

35&36   An ambience, like a district, can make a very
memorable place to which you are eager to
return. Whereas districts are bounded by
physical borders, ambiences are bounded by
a certain quality of space, such as the filtered
green light under the trees of an oasis in
Palermo, Italy, or the screened-in porch of
our House near Washington, DC.

32

33

34

35

36

37

38

39

37–40   An ambience can be collected in a place, as
        when the morning sun fills the east-facing
        Piazzetta di San Marco in Venice, Italy (37)
        or the courtyard of the Reid House I in
        Cleveland Heights, Ohio (40). Similarly,
        cooling breezes are collected on the hilltops
        of Ravello, Italy (38), or in the writer's perch
        of the Crowell Studio on Long Island,
        New York (39).

41–42   Ambiences can also emanate from a source
        such as the cooling breezes from a fountain
        or the warmth and glow from the fireplace of
        our House in the Hudson Valley.

40

41

42

43

44

43&44 Smell is a powerful creator of ambience.
Who does not recall the aroma of freshly
baked bread from the local bakery? The
fragrances of an herb garden fill the small
entry court of the House in the Hudson
Valley.

45–47 Sound is another component of ambience.
In Istanbul, Turkey, the call to prayer
emanating from the minarets permeates the
city. Whether emanating from a source or
trapped within a space, sound can create a
memorable place and orient the wanderer.
The stone mass of the bar room in the
Guyott House creates a hushed ambience
that makes the room distinctive. The brightly
tiled fountain in the main stair hall of the
House near New York can be heard
throughout the house and helps to
orient its blind owner.

45

46

47

Emotional Impact

Villages can have an emotional impact upon us that is both enticing and memorable. It happens as we move through their streets and piazzas. We respond to contrasts, such as when a confined space opens dramatically into a wide, open one. We like paths that take us on mysterious adventures. Passing over a threshold to leave one world and enter another can be magical. Also, the contents of a village can intrigue us, move us to tears, or can fill us with joy and make us laugh.

48

49

50

48&49   The contrast of the immediate view in front of us linked to an emerging view adds interest and mystery to the village streets of Palermo, Italy and also to the Reid House I dining room as it connects to the kitchen and den beyond.

50&51   A sense of threshold—that is, a sense of leaving one world and entering another, as one does when entering San Marco Piazza in Venice—has a powerfully emotional impact. The Reid House I is on a noisy road in Cleveland Heights, Ohio and is surrounded by houses about 20 feet away on its three other sides. But walking through the gateway into the courtyard creates the feeling of having arrived in a far-off place. The birds chirp, the flowers are fragrant, and the grass is soft and green. The passage through the gate offers a remarkable change.

51

52

53

52–55　Like the canyon road leading to the ancient city of Petra, an oasis in the desert of Jordan, the threshold experience at the Acheson House is dramatized by a carefully orchestrated procession. A boardwalk leads to a gateway that ushers you to the front door then through a passageway that separates the main house from the guest house.

56–58　Finally, just as a magnificent view of Petra once unfolded to ancient caravans, a deck, pool, and panorama of the Connecticut River emerge at the end of the boardwalk.

54

55

56

57

58

59

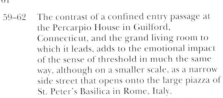

61

60

59–62 The contrast of a confined entry passage at the Percarpio House in Guilford, Connecticut, and the grand living room to which it leads, adds to the emotional impact of the sense of threshold in much the same way, although on a smaller scale, as a narrow side street that opens onto the large piazza of St. Peter's Basilica in Rome, Italy.

63–66 There is a special, emotional impact in an ascent to a high place, such as at the Acropolis in Athens, Greece (63& 65). At the Reid House II on Cape Cod, Massachusetts (64&66), steps lead to the second-floor living room where broad views of the ocean dramatically unfold with each step. The tops of the windows are set low, accentuating a sense of the room's height and urging you to sit down and stay awhile.

62

63

64

65

66

67&69   Being below the general ground plane, as
        one often is in the coastal towns of the
        Algarve in Portugal, generates an emotional
        reaction quite different to one's reaction to
        being above the ground plane, as on the
        bridges of Paris.

68&70   From the great room of the House in the
        Hudson Valley, you look up to the bunk
        room, which is perched like a tree house in
        the branches of the columns. From above,
        the bunk room overlooks the great room.

67

68

69

70

71

72

73

74

71–74   The contents of a village also create
         emotional impact. They tell us things of
         interest about the place and give it character.
         Just as the contents of the Magic Kingdom at
         Disney World (71) tell about an age gone by,
         the stairway of the Pall Corporation in Port
         Washington (74) is adorned with a coil of
         stainless steel, which informs us about the
         materials used in the manufacturing of their
         products. At Quinnipiac College, the same
         type of microphones used in the first Johnny
         Carson Shows adorn the Ed McMahon Mass
         Communication Center (72). At the
         Quinnipiac College School of Law Center,
         "open book" wall sconces are inscribed with
         words of wisdom, advice, and reassurance for
         young lawyers (73).

75

76

75–77 & Following page:
Vibrant colors can lift our spirits. The important lesson villages teach is that bold use of color can be not only acceptable, but a virtue. At the Wriston Art Center (77 & following page), color was used to contrast with the predominately beige stone veneer of the campus and provide an emotional lift during the long, bleak winter months of northern Wisconsin. Likewise, the Winter Garden at the Cedar Rapids Art Museum (75) is bold in the use of color, to get you through the winter in high spirits.

77

79&80   Materials that carry meaningful associations generate strong emotional reactions. At the Striar Jewish Community Center, our charge was to make a center for all Jews, both religious and non-religious. We suggested building the Center's courtyard with the famous Jerusalem stone. This is the very same stone used by Herod to build the second Jewish Temple, the remaining base of which is Jerusalem's famous Wailing Wall, and also used by dictum throughout the city. It symbolizes, at once, all facets of Judaism.

Sociability

Villages are sociable places partly because
they have a concentration of people and
activities, but also because of the way they
are built. Delightful places to sit, places
that we pass by and peer into, the ability to
display our things, the offering of food,
access to water, a reflection of our human
scale, and settings for public celebration
all work in villages to attract people, make
them feel sociable, and encourage their
interaction.

81

82

83

81&82   William H. Whyte made the straightforward observation that if you want people to sit and stay awhile, you need to provide places for them to sit. Yet, it is amazing how much effort is made to prevent people from sitting down and enjoying themselves; witness one device commonly used in New York City. At the Carl Hansen Student Center at Quinnipiac College, as in all of our work, we have taken small opportunities everywhere to make seats.

83&84   Of course, sitting in groups of people is fun, too, a fact to which anyone who has been to the Spanish Steps in Rome can attest. Below, students sit in the outdoor café within the courtyard of Quinnipiac College's School of Law Center.

84

85

85–88   People especially like to sit on the edge of a
path where they can watch the world go by.
At the Colby College Student Center, the
post office lounge is enclosed by double-
hung windows that open onto the main
campus path, which passes through the
building; students sit here and watch or
engage passersby. The lounge is like a small
terrace overlooking the Grand Canal in
Venice, Italy.

86

87

88

89

90

91

92

89–92 People also like to sit in sunshine. In many villages, such as this one in
Mykonos, Greece (90), we find both large and small sun traps, or places
that protect you from the wind and trap the sun. Similarly, the Colby
College Student Center (89) spreads its wings to trap the sun and block the
north wind on the entrance side of the building. Even on sunny winter
days, the outdoor terraces are inviting. Likewise, the pavilions that join to
make up the Pond House (92), set on a wind-blown coastline, make way for
a smaller, but no less welcome sun trap. At Quinnipiac College (91) we
built sun traps between the existing buildings.

93

94

95

93–96   The ability to peer into a place of activity as
you pass it by enhances a village's image of
sociability, as this small alley at Disney World
illustrates (94). The great room at Colby
College's Student Center also reveals itself to
the rest of the campus (95). At the Wriston
Art Center, passersby can peer into the lower-
level studios or view student art displayed
along interior exhibit walls (96). The
Sanctuary for the Headquarters of the
United Church of Christ in the old Ohio Bell
Building in Cleveland, Ohio (93) can be
viewed by passersby on Prospect Avenue, as
well as by guests in our new hotel and garden
courtyard. This fulfills the liturgical goal of
connecting the church to life here on earth.

96

97

99

100

98

97–100 Accommodating the human urge to display the things we cherish or are proud of adds visibly to the sociability of a place. Merchants proudly display their craft work in Istanbul, Turkey (99). The dining room of the Reid House I is seen as you enter through the courtyard and displays the owner's special collection of Mexican artifacts (97&98). At the Taplin House, we made a center chimney inexpensively out of concrete blocks alternately indented to receive tiles (100). A custom was then established within the family and among friends that house gifts would be colorful tiles from travels or favorite artists to adorn the chimney mass and transform it over time into a talisman of friendship and fond memories.

101–103 Places with trees are especially attractive to people. We are biologically made for the forest, with our eyesight favoring the dappled light under a canopy of leaves. But, also, trees can figuratively populate a place in much the same way as people do. The palm trees in the courtyard of our Norton Museum of Art, West Palm Beach, Florida are a major reason people are attracted to this place (102). Well-pruned trees in a parking lot in Chambord, France are as playful as people (103), while trees on a hillside street in Italy seem almost to be walking down hill (101).

104&105 Food is also a great way to attract people. At the Carl Hansen Student Center café, tables are placed along the curving edge of a hallway to enliven it.

103

101

104

102

106&107　Water is another great attracter of people, but its attraction comes from the ability to touch it and play with it. So access to the water, as provided along the river's edge in Lucern, Switzerland, is what is most important. Our freeze–thaw fountain at the Wriston Art Center in northern Wisconsin brings sluices of water out to its edges, where people can touch it. The fountain converts to steam in the late fall, building up a large ice sculpture throughout the winter, which then ceremoniously melts with the coming of spring.

108&109　At the Striar Jewish Community Center, a drinking fountain outside the gym becomes a place where people linger and chat, not unlike the fountain at the Spanish Steps in Rome.

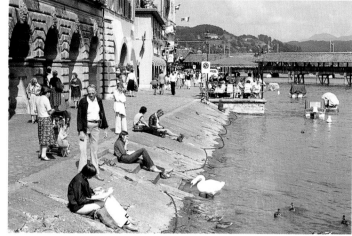

106

107

108

109

110–112

The ways in which a place such as the Campidoglio in Rome relate to the size and shape of our bodies also play a part in how welcome and comfortable we feel there. The magic of Disneyland's Magic Kingdom happens in part because of its reduced scale. At our Wriston Art Center, the human scale of the building is one of its main attractions.

110

111

112

113

116

117

114

113–115
Evidence of the human hand being involved, as can be seen in Banares, India (113) adds to the feeling that a place is for people. At our Elliott House in Ligonier, Pennsylvania (114), the artist–owner and architect collaborated on a hand-etched plaster wall used to store solar heat. A hand-stenciled design on the walls of Quinnipiac College's Computer Center helps to humanize the space (115).

116&117
Surfaces that are worn from use, such as the columns of this temple in Kyoto, Japan, suggest the passage of people before us and a promise that others will follow, giving us a sense of the human continuum. At the Carl Hansen Student Center, limestone benches in the "Agora" were designed to take on a patina that would show years of use.

115

118

119

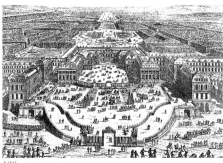

120

121

122

118&119   Some of the most important settings for
          social interaction are the outdoor spaces,
          large and small, that are formed between
          our buildings. It is from these nooks,
          piazzas, and courtyards found in villages
          that we can learn many lessons about
          sociability for our single buildings.
          However, many American buildings,
          especially our colleges and universities,
          stand alone as single objects and speak of
          independence. Indeed, the typical
          American dream house stands apart, even
          when it makes no sense to do so, as in
          Levittown, New York.

   120   Yet, in Europe, an entirely different
          attitude brings people together in
          courtyards and piazzas as settings for
          public life. Indeed, in earlier times the
          term "courtyard" referred to the yard in
          which the court met and conducted its
          public business, as this etching of
          Versailles illustrates.

121&122   Today, people flock to outdoor enclaves
          such as the piazza in front of the Pantheon
          in Rome. At our Quinnipiac College
          School of Law Center, its four wings
          enclose a courtyard which is not only used
          sociably but also is intended to symbolize
          the value of a public life. This area is
          transformed, periodically, into a place for
          community celebrations.

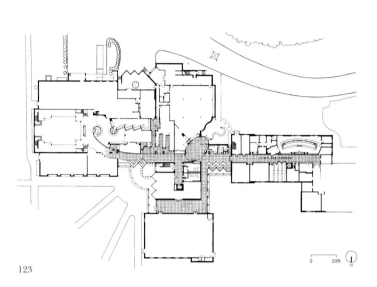

123

124

125

123–125   One of the keys to the success of such
community celebration spaces is, as the
research of my partner Chad Floyd
establishes, the creation of an enclave. An
enclave is a protected, enclosed space. It is
often most effective when carved out of a
network of activity. Like the piazza in
Lucca, Italy (124), the "Agora" at the Carl
Hansen Student Center offers a haven in
the hub-bub (123&125).

126–129   Enclaves, such as Il Campo in Siena, Italy
(126), are especially effective as social
places when they are shaped in a curve so
that people can see the faces of other
people. The curved shape of the Grand
Court Room at the Quinnipiac College Law
School Center serves an alternate function
as an interactive classroom (127). The
indoor–outdoor theater of the Stepping
Stones Museum for Children opens to a
semi-circular spectators' lawn enclosed by a
curved pergola (128&129).

126

127

128

129

130

131

132

133

130&131 Another essential key for public celebration spaces is the provision of a talisman or focal point to act as a backdrop for pageantry. Cinderella's castle in Disney World's Magic Kingdom is a dramatic illustration. Stairs and railings descending from a balcony at the far end of the dining hall of the Carl Hansen Student Center at Quinnipiac College create such a talisman—they act as the proscenium for impromptu gigs, speeches, and small events conducted throughout the week.

132&133 Once enclave and talisman are combined and working together, the key is to make them work in some routine mode so that they never appear as an empty stage casting a forlorn mood over the place when not being used. The County Courthouse in Santa Barbara, California served as a model for the Colby College Student Center. Like the Courthouse, which functions routinely as a civic building and on occasion is transformed into a setting for celebration, the banquettes in the Student Center routinely provide places to eat in the "Pub", but on Friday nights they are transformed into a stage for performances of all sorts.

134&135   The base of the existing library tower at Quinnipiac College was given a new arched, brick veneer and a semi-circular plinth of granite steps. In the routine mode they serve as seats and as a distinguished entry to the library, but on occasion the steps become a stage, and the brick arch a talisman for concerts, ceremonies, and other student events.

136&137   A routine ramp connecting two levels of the piazza at the Quinnipiac College Dormitory (136) is transformed on Friday and Saturday nights into a setting for celebration. The Wriston amphitheater (137) is a place for casual sitting or for viewing the artists' studios within. With the addition of theater lights on portable stanchions set into sleeves at the upper level, it is easily transformed into an outdoor theater or celebration space.

134

135

136

137

Chapter 16 The Dartmouth Gamble

Chad Floyd

Dartmouth College is the quintessential old American campus, a collegiate haven where buildings share loose, pleasing, and mostly Georgian agreements around an elm-lined green.

Hanging in a spot in the College's Facilities Planning Department, where everyone will be sure to see it, is a handsome certificate awarded to Dartmouth some years ago by the New Hampshire Chapter of the American Institute of Architects. The certificate praises the College for having shown intellectual leadership by introducing to its campus a number of progressive new buildings. Next to the certificate, Dartmouth's staff of facility administrators and architects has placed a photograph of one of the buildings to which the certificate refers.

The building is a two-story affair, startlingly different from the College's traditional architecture. It has a flat roof and a featureless gray façade with mill-finished aluminum windows set in horizontal bands. Standing in front of the façade is a slightly curved, two-story panel, clad with tiles in a checkerboard of turquoise and blue.

The building, which houses the math department, departs bravely from the norms of Georgian architecture surrounding it. It is a perfectly fine, inexpensive, functional building, and some might even consider it stylish. Over the 20 or so years since the building's construction, enough time has passed for the college community to form a universal judgment of it. The judgment is aptly expressed by the certificate's location. It is placed, not in the corridor among other projects completed by the Facilities Planning Department, but in the bathroom, where it is remembered as a mistake.

What Dartmouth has come to believe is that its distinguished old campus should, on the whole, be protected from buildings, especially background buildings, that depart excessively from the norm. The risks are considered to be too great.

This is a conservative view, but it comes from experience over post-war years with buildings that paid little heed to the fabric of the campus, with results the Dartmouth community now considers disastrous. The College's gamble, which seems to me to be reasonable for such a distinguished place, is that it is better to require architects to follow the campus's established warp and weft, than to allow overly personal statements. The staff of Dartmouth's Facilities Planning Department has only to visit the bathroom to recall how today's refreshing departure may be tomorrow's discordant note.

Dartmouth is not doctrinaire about this. The College acknowledges that, even in its historic confines, there are some sites and building types that call for contemporary expression, but such opportunities are viewed as rare. The governing rule is a set of conditions by which architects' contributions to the campus are meant to make its whole continue to exceed the sum of its parts.

If Dartmouth's gamble succeeds, what of other places? To what extent should we be concentrating on contextural wholeness, rather than lavishing attention on buildings as objects?

College campuses may be a focus for this controversy, but in a broader sense they are set apart from it. Since most American college campuses date from the 19th century, and sometimes even earlier, they are rich in older buildings when compared with newer corporate, residential, and industrial campuses. This makes them less relevant to the larger debate, which is framed as a choice between maintaining a continuum of historical forms, or creating a vital and diverse expression of the evolving culture. Indeed, for Dartmouth, that framing truly misses the point. What Dartmouth and many of her sister institutions seek is not idealization of the past, but visual order, plain and simple. Dartmouth's preference for traditional forms is nothing more than an acknowledgement of buildings already present, salted with a belief that traditional forms tend to promote pleasing campus relationships—certainly as pleasing as anything else architects have come up with lately.

This raises interesting questions about the limited success we architects have had in creating places over time that sustain visual sense. It also suggests that historic colleges such as Dartmouth will continue to build in the old ways.

1

2

CITATION

*Founded in 1769, **Dartmouth College** is justly proud of its long New England tradition. Dartmouth Row reflects in the simplicity of its architecture this rich Colonial heritage, and newer buildings of Georgian style have continued to demonstrate appropriately Dartmouth's identity with New England's early history.*

That tradition, however deeply rooted in the past, need not impede progress is evidenced by Dartmouth's record of accomplishment and leadership in the field of education. Recently the college has given further evidence of its forward-looking attitude by introducing within its campus new buildings of contemporary design. It is not important on this occasion that professional people agree on the quality of the designs, but it is important that Dartmouth is creating opportunities for the expression of new and stimulating architecture. The influence of Dartmouth's new architecture upon the aesthetic sensitivity of New Hampshire's citizens is significant.

*For this contribution to the creation of a climate favorable to the stimulation of better architecture, the New Hampshire Chapter of the American Institute of Architects is pleased to present to **Dartmouth College** this citation.*

3

1 Dartmouth Hall, with its landmark Georgian cupola and copper roofs, fronts the famous Dartmouth Green.
2 Among the new buildings cited by the AIA was Bradley-Gerry, a departure from the Dartmouth norm. It is regarded by Dartmouth's Facilities Planning Department as discordant.
3 In the 1970s, the New Hampshire Chapter of the AIA cited Dartmouth for introducing contemporary architecture into its Georgian campus.
4 Dartmouth College, the quintessential American campus, is exemplified by Baker Library.

4

5

6

7

5 Our 1985 Hood Museum of Art at Dartmouth College refers to New England mill architecture, but is comfortable with the copper gables and red brick of Dartmouth's traditional buildings.

6&7 For intimate scale, Centerbrook's 1991 Byrne Hall at Dartmouth's Tuck School of Business has a lower eave than most buildings on campus, but it uses Dartmouth's neo-Georgian vernacular of white-painted accents within a brick frame and sloped slate roofs. Byrne Hall's entry door is the focus of a new courtyard that is considered almost as important as the building itself.

8

9

10

8   Centerbrook's new Art and Art History Building at Colgate University uses the campus's established language of stone buildings, yet makes a courtyard that steps down a steep hill in a manner new to the Colgate campus.

9   At the University of Toledo, crisp anodized aluminum is our material, but this new 400-bed dormitory helps to make a coherent whole by stitching itself to the campus's Gothic character.

10 The Centennial Building at Pomfret School shares neo-Georgian character with its neighbors without imitating them.

11

11 Over a 12-year period, we have transformed an aging 53-acre plant in Groton, Connecticut, into a modern pharmaceutical manufacturing facility for Pfizer. Although industrial, the plant is, in effect, a campus and has been treated as such. The architecture is technological and Modernist. Visual order is achieved by painting everything that is curved, old or new, bright white (pipe racks, tanks, and the like) and all else beige. A sense of unity results.

12 The Pfizer Administration Building canopy is a beige foreground to a long, curving white gateway to the plant in the distance.

13 Our Technology Building at Pfizer illustrates the benefit of a universally followed plan. Since it is rectangular, the building is beige. It is sharply juxtaposed against the white pipes and cylinders of a tank farm.

12

13

Chapter 17 Buildings as Friends

Mark Simon

Some of my best friends are buildings.

We are all mortal. The thought of death scares most of us and makes us feel alone. The connections we make with other people are an antidote to this feeling. Though family is most important, colleagues, friends, and our fellows in society also ease a fearful solitude. We make connections with all of them by communicating—giving and loving, expressing ourselves, working, playing. Empathy is particularly satisfying, since by understanding the needs and feelings of others, we feel connected to them because we share their humanity, and they, perhaps, ours. We can employ that in making architecture to soothe others and ourselves at the same time. Buildings, when cared for, care for us and accompany us. They make us feel less alone. They can be among our best friends.

How do we empathize in architecture? We architects can listen carefully to our clients to learn their dreams and needs. They do not always know what they want, or know how to express it, so we often have to go to lengths to draw it out of them. Then we transform their visions into buildings. The buildings thus recognize and converse with their occupants.

We are all fragile; except for the most skilled survivalists, we would not thrive alone in nature. Buildings provide shelter in a symbiotic relationship. We keep them tight; they keep us dry. But this physical *quid pro quo* is not really a satisfying conversation, one that provides us with psychological shelter. When the building *tells* us that it will provide shelter, then we might hear the building speak. Overhanging roofs, deep set windows, and durable materials all tell us that we are sheltered. They help us *feel* protected.

Buildings also recognize their occupants in their commodity, with the proper arrangement of spaces and convenience. If this is specific to particular users, they sense the friendship all the more. People truly enjoy a place that was made "just for them". It might be as simple as furniture designed to meet their personal needs, or a place might commemorate their activities or honor their passions. A building's entrance can say "hello".

Buildings engage us with meaningful memories, or the signs of habitation that Donlyn Lyndon of Moore, Lyndon, Turnbull, Whitaker has written about. Buildings speak with symbols and signs, or even with figurative elements like "faces" or bodies.

Sometimes, buildings might even amuse and entertain us, like our favorite friends. They can make us laugh, or may even thrill us from time to time.

1

2

3

4

4 The landscaped courtyard at the Pond House greets cars, not as utilitarian vehicles, but as welcome guests.

5 The carefully designed study at the Pond House is built to meet all the professor's needs, both with its built-in furniture and its viewing windows.

6&7 Interior windows at the Eisenstein House and balconies at the Quinnipiac College School of Law Center suggest the people who might stand at them. We feel accompanied.

5

6

7

8

9

10

8 The screened porch in a Private Residence in Connecticut is a safe meeting
point with nature. Breezes and scents enter; bugs and rain stay out.

9 The porte-cochère at the McKim House welcomes and protects visitors.

10 Deep-set windows and entry porches give this new Science Building at
Cheshire Academy a sense of permanence and shelter.

Opposite:
Brick arches at Quinnipiac College's School of Business Center invite entry
and offer refuge.

13

14

12   Buildings can thrill. In order to heighten excitement on the way to exhibits, the sloping people-mover at Nauticus, the National Maritime Center, tunnels up through changing bulkheads and offers occasional glimpses to the harbor life far below.

13   The waving entry canopy and warm lighting at Brandeis's Shapiro Admissions Center both welcomes and protects visitors.

14   Monumental piers and arches excite visitors as entry "gangplanks" lead them over the water they are about to explore inside Nauticus's exhibits.

15&16   The ultimate commodity is a place you can change to your own taste. The showroom for New Hearth in New York allows visitors to form their own kitchen mock-ups with rolling counters and kitchen equipment on a measuring floor.

17   The staff at PricewaterhouseCoopers Kwasha HR Solutions are amused each day with an entrance to their offices through a hallway of neon and glass.

18   The Lego Imagination Center at Disney World entertains visitors with over-scaled bricks, flying figures, and a starry ceiling.

15

16

17

18

Chapter 18 Finding the Genetic Code

Jim Childress

We have worked at Cold Spring Harbor Laboratory in Cold Spring Harbor, New York for over 25 years. The laboratory is an international center for research of molecular biology. The scientists there are hard at work unraveling the genetic code in human DNA in an attempt to understand why we humans are the way we are. There is a parallel between their work and architecture. In a similar way, architects must find the "genes" that will give form and spirit to a building. These "genes" come from many sources and many parts of the world and seldom from the place where we are building. When assembled properly, they will create a unique building that has a recognizable and meaningful relation to its progenitors.

Architects are trained in school and pressured by their peers to create unique designs that express their individuality.

Simultaneously, architects are challenged to respond to the history and essence of a place. These are both important aspects of design, one drawing inspiration from the self and the other from the place. But I am most enthusiastic about drawing inspiration from the people who will inhabit the place. I want to find the genetic code of a building.

In America there is a mix of many cultures and nationalities. Simply responding to the history or climate of a particular place does not by itself relate a building in meaningful ways to its users. The people who inhabit our buildings are far more diverse than the context in which they reside. Each has inherited a different history.

Cold Spring Harbor Laboratory has grown as an institution well beyond its

beginnings as the Columbia University summer biology camp located on a residential estate on Long Island. Although it has always been important that the buildings we design there fit comfortably in their existing residential setting, it is equally important that they reflect the influence of the board of directors, composed of many individuals with diverse backgrounds; that they respond to the aspirations of its Director, Nobel Laureate James D. Watson, educated in part at Cambridge University; and that they answer to the new Director, Bruce Stillman, who comes from Australia and brings yet another viewpoint. These are a few of the many people who have each added a gene, more or less dominant, to the character formation or "genetic code" of the Laboratory.

1

1 On the north shore of Long Island, New York, Cold Spring Harbor Laboratory has grown from a summer camp for biology to an international center for molecular biology and genetic research. The open space and manicured grounds have been influenced by Director James D. Watson's memories of landscapes around Cambridge, England, where he studied.

2 The design of the Neuroscience Center at Cold Spring Harbor Laboratory and its bell tower, among the first brick buildings on the campus, was influenced by scientists who had come to the Laboratory from colleges and universities throughout the United States and England.

3 The house for Dr. and Mrs. Watson blends American sensibilities with the influence of Dr. Watson's years in England.

2

3

Each project requires a fresh start in order to make it the unique offspring of a set of "genes" or influences specific to its owner or users. Too many "genes" from someone else's building are likely to yield a stranger to the client. Yet, adapting afresh to every new project poses a challenge. The lack of repetition makes it difficult to refine details. Many noted architects, such as Richard Meier and Mario Botta, whose designs are each a part of a singular and personal lifelong quest, can develop over time well-rehearsed and, consequently, elegant and refined ways in which to insert windows into walls, to turn corners, construct glazing systems, extend soffits, and so on. The challenge we face is that, by designing unique projects, we have many opportunities to invent but few of the opportunities architects such as Meier and Botta have to perfect.

This approach of looking at each project with fresh eyes is not solely due to a design conviction. To be honest, it also comes from being restless and not wanting to do one thing repeatedly. It is more exciting to discover new ways to do things.

I worry, in this light, that a building that adheres so closely to the stated desires and influences of its clients, may yield a structure that is so specialized and so defined by what the users know and understand about themselves, that discovery by them of the remainder of their "genetic make-up", of which they may be unaware, is made impossible. The same problem is faced by genetic engineers who set out to create, say, a consistently perfect tomato, one that is perfectly red and grows perfectly fast. They try to eliminate the "junk genes", those that do not appear to contribute to the pre-defined perfection. The danger is that the junk gene, which was engineered out, may, in fact, be the one needed in the future to offset the onslaught of some unpredicted disease or, conversely, to take advantage of some unpredicted windfall. The lesson for architects might be that we could benefit our clients by taking the design of their building beyond the evident and the prescribable to areas of satisfaction for them which are understood by us only by intuition and accessed by them only by discovery.

4

5

Every project we approach has clues to its genetic code. Each clue, if you follow it, leads to a gene that will make it possible to create a unique building, imbued with meaning for those who will live and work there.

4   For the Luke Building at Cold Spring Harbor Laboratory, the detailing responds to the building committee's fondness of traditional wood buildings, while adding subtle new twists.

5   The all-new interior reflects the same attitude as the exterior—a blend of new images with imagined traditional ones.

6   This renovation of the Erle House on the Connecticut shore reflects its owner's Japanese heritage, many years of world travel, and 20 years of living in rural Connecticut.

7   The interior, with the Japanese elements of wood joinery and fabric panels, reflects the owner's love of the violin (note the curves in the ceiling that mimic those of a violin) and her deep-rooted interest in nature.

6

7

206 Enthusiasms of Centerbrook

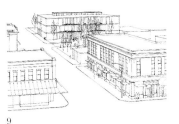

9

10

11

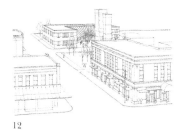

12

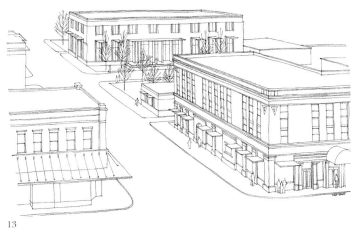

13

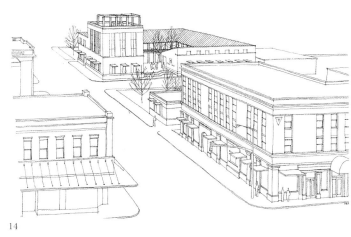

14

15

8   A table for four very active kids and their friends is given an energetic look.

9–15   During the design of the headquarters for the National Outdoor Leadership School (NOLS) in Lander, Wyoming, multiple options were explored to discover its "genetic code." The building needed to respond to its neighborhood, the city, the region, and to the unique character of the people who make up the organization. Schemes were eliminated or adopted based on how well the image conveyed a sense of frugality, humility, community, worldliness, common sense, and responsibility to the environment.

  9   The Bar Ranch Scheme
  10   The Double Bar Ranch Scheme
  11   The Cirque of the Towers Scheme
  12   The Brand "L" Scheme
  13   The Bar Ranch 2 Scheme
  14   The Double Bar Ranch 2 Scheme
  15   The Final Scheme

16   The additions flanking the historic Heckscher Museum of Art in Huntington, New York, respond to a number of influences. The trellis-like wings maintain the lines of the original building for those who are traditional. The symmetry answers to those who want a place of stature to attract visitors. The glass inserts of the wings recede into the surrounding park to satisfy the people who treasure the landscape.

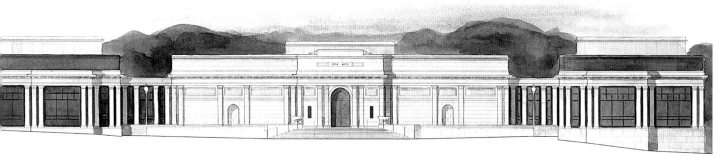

16

17

19

18

20

17&18   The addition to the Trudeau Institute in Saranac Lake, New York, maintains the scientific character that the original laboratory brought to this remote part of the Adirondacks. The ecological concerns of the current director and staff also influenced the way in which the addition connects to its natural setting. The building gently bends to claim the hilltop and capture views of Saranac Lake and the Adirondack Mountains beyond.

19   The conference room acts as a social hinge between the addition and the original building. The concrete columns mimic the original entry, but are set in visual motion, reflecting the rapid change of research. The upper porch becomes a rock outcropping overlooking the lake below.

20   A fire stair is configured to allow playful interaction.

21   An open connection between the new and old buildings is a frugal solution to providing a sun-filled central meeting area intended to foster communication throughout the whole Institute.

22   The remote side adds an element of discovery as it bends with the hill and leads to a bay window, the design of which merges with the trees.

21

22

Chapter 19 Getting Out of the Toolbox

Bill Grover

While working at General Motors, I was asked to design a pattern for the glass door of an electric range. The idea was that the pattern would somewhat obscure the inside of the oven but, when an interior light was turned on, would still allow the chef to look inside to see how the roast was progressing. Seven or eight designers were set to the task, and each was asked to come up, within a few days, with ten patterns to show the boss.

The drawing tools at our disposal at that time were pencils, pens, parallel straight edges, triangles, compasses, circle and ellipse guides, and other plastic curve devices. Not surprisingly, almost all the patterns consisted of straight lines, circles, diagonals, and curves that could be easily constructed with the tools at hand. It occurred to me at that time what a strong influence the tools have on the design. I decided to look for different tools. Using a borrowed oscilloscope and two signal generators from the engineering department, I made some unusual figures on the screen, photographed and replicated them to make patterns, none of which could have been conceived easily using traditional drafting tools.

There were no speedy drafting computers at that time, and representation of three-dimensional forms was difficult and time consuming. Representations of compound, curved surfaces were left to sculptors and model builders who translated designers' two-dimensional sketches into clay models. When refined, these models were subsequently measured and then (in the case of automobiles) cut by pattern makers into the steel dies that stamped out sheet metal.

Now that architects and industrial designers have access to sophisticated computers that can draw, illustrate, and carve out almost any conceivable form, the character of architecture is changing. Frank Gehry's spectacular recent buildings would not be possible without these new tools. Alas, because it is becoming so easy, Frank will have to suffer seeing badly crafted, knock-off versions of his concepts dotting the landscape.

1

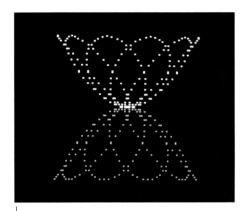

2

3

1 "ORNAMAT" computer program for use in the design of architectural ornament, 1979.
2 "Chemical architecture." Free-form houses at Yale were made in 1967 of expanded polyurethane foam sprayed on inflatable forms.
3 Modern computer tools allow us to view designs for complicated structures and lighting effects from any vantage point, as in this conference room for the University of Connecticut Business School.
4 Stenciled graphics were generated on our first computer for the Quinnipiac College Computer Center.

4

Chapter 20 Making Television Useful

Chad Floyd

In an attempt to distinguish Centerbrook from better-qualified firms competing for a planning project in Ohio, we managed to invent a new use for television. The idea helped us get the job, suggesting that necessity is indeed the mother of invention.

The job was to redesign the Great Miami River as it flows through Dayton, Ohio. The date was 1976. An attempt by the City a year earlier to plan a downtown riverfront plaza had been rejected by voters. Not wanting to repeat the mistake, the City of Dayton was keen on involving citizens the second time around.

Hoping our competitors would be over-confident, we stretched ourselves by offering to staff a project office in a downtown storefront. The City was so impressed it made our idea a prerequisite for all the competing firms. The wind in our sails thus depleted, we knew we had to step up our proposal a notch. So the idea came to us to offer to do the job live on TV. We thought no other firm would consider such a hare-brained approach, and we were indeed right.

So we approached Dayton's PBS station, and, frankly, were surprised to find it interested and actually willing to produce the programs. Before long, our proposal for using television had been accepted by the City, and we were propelled into the world of popular media.

Eventually, we produced six shows in Dayton. They were broadcast live during prime time on Thursday nights. Our idea was to make the programs interactive, so that people could call in with their ideas. What emerged was an odd cross between a Jerry Lewis Telethon and "Let's Make a Deal". A local television personality was assigned to represent John Q. Public and, essentially, to ask elementary questions, which he did with verve. The urban plan that evolved on our "Design-a-Thons", as they came to be known, was eventually approved by the community, and Centerbrook's version of the previous year's riverfront plaza advanced swiftly to implementation.

We were so impressed with television's potential for planning, that we went on in the late 1970s and 1980s to produce 16 more hours of shows, all of them for prime time viewing and on commercial stations which have much greater numbers of viewers. Our very next series (we began to think of our projects in "I Love Lucy" terms) was for the revitalization of downtown Roanoke, Virginia, the largest urban center in southwest Virginia. Our station, Roanoke's CBS affiliate, was the biggest market in the mid-Atlantic area, after Washington, DC. It offered blanket coverage of southwestern Virginia and North Carolina.

1

2

3

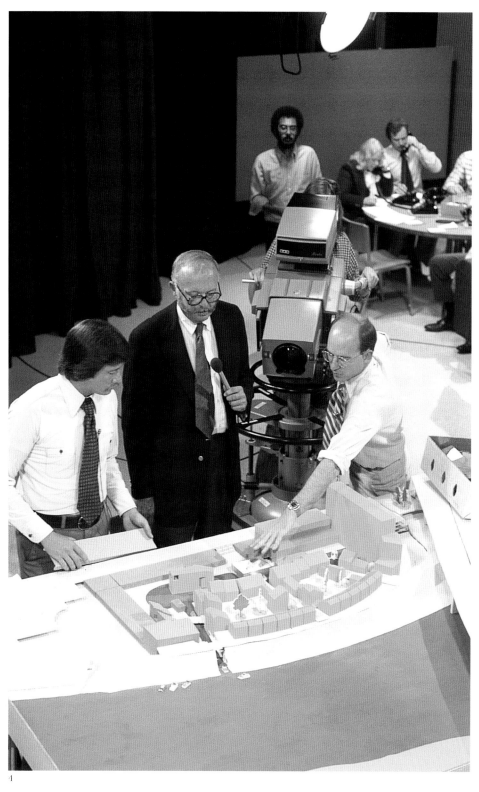

1 The backbone of the TV process is the citizens'
group, which collaborates with us in workshops.
In 1980, the Watkins Glen citizens' group toured
the waterfront and answered questions in their
notebooks.
2 Chad Floyd collects riverfront comments in the
Dayton, Ohio, storefront office in 1976.
3 Rich Hackney, TV personality in Dayton, left,
stands in as surrogate for the public.
4 Steve Carter (of Lorenz and Williams), Charles
Moore, and Chad Floyd demonstrate the finer
points of a waterfront housing proposal before a
live camera (Dayton, Ohio, 1976).

4

We did four hours of Roanoke shows, again for prime-time viewing. Here, too, our commission followed a downtown plan that was gathering dust for lack of community support. For us, getting the attention of the community would be no problem, as our TV shows were reaching 90,000 people a night. I found it remarkable to run into strangers the day after a show and find myself asked knowledgeable questions about issues unveiled only the night before.

The Roanoke master plan repositioned that city's downtown as the social and cultural center of the community, but did so in ways startling to some. These included uprooting four of the city's premier cultural institutions from stately suburban locales and co-locating them in a promising but dilapidated market area favored at night by the local transvestite population. Initially resisted by the movers and shakers, our plan eventually became so popular it was presented to City Council not by us but by our citizen telephone respondents. Funding for public elements was subsequently approved in a referendum by an impressive margin. There then ensued an intense five-year period during which we were kept busy implementing the plan's public, and even some of its private, proposals.

After Roanoke, Centerbrook partner Mark Simon joined me in Springfield, Massachusetts, for a project on yet another riverfront. By this time we had gained a track record, and the television stations pretty much left us to produce the shows on our own. It was in Springfield that our production values advanced to a higher level. Mark and I realized that our shows needed to be better centered, so we lost the local television personality and placed ourselves at a desk at the center of the studio, from which we conducted

interviews and anchored the hour. We even brought in kids from the community to carry copies of viewer suggestions to key points in the studio. And, as he had done in our previous TV shows, partner Jeff Riley worked his magic at the drawing board, visualizing callers' ideas with instant sketches. To some viewers, seeing Jeff's sketches come alive in a few strokes was something akin to a miracle.

After Springfield, we went on to Watkins Glen, New York; Indianapolis (as advisers to Charles Moore, who was undertaking a project there with HNTB); and eventually back to Virginia to master plan, with Jones and Jones of Seattle, a cultural theme park telling the story of the Lewis and Clark Expedition.

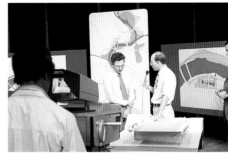

5

6

7

5   In a later show in Dayton, Ohio (1 of 6), I interviewed City Traffic Engineer Joe Stemley on the air and elicited a promise to revert a lane of bridge traffic to pedestrians.

6   A steering committee of movers and shakers from private and public sectors is a staple of Centerbrook's TV planning. The downtown Roanoke, Virginia, committee at work in 1978.

7   Participants from the citizens' group staff busy phones in Roanoke's fall 1978 show.

8   Jeff Riley shows his sketching stuff at a drafting table used to visualize callers' concepts. Neighborhood children act as runners.

9   Mark Simon joins Chad Floyd in 1980 to co-host a series of three shows in Springfield, Massachusetts. This is where we discovered the centering effect of an anchor desk.

By the mid-1980s we had tuned our "Design-a-Thons" into a passably professional, though certainly not slick, standard. We had become proficient at conceiving and producing complicated, hour-long television shows and had shown them to be powerful tools for involving citizens in their communities. We were featured on the CBS Morning News; I wrote a couple of articles about our experiences, and we looked forward to seeing architects across the land begin shaping the public realm in prime time.

8

9

It never happened. The Reagan administration removed most of the funding vehicles that had been in place for public works projects under Jimmy Carter, and in the 1980s communities literally stopped planning. Also, it seemed architects just didn't take well to our "Design-a-Thon" concept. When a professor at the Yale Architecture School suggested a design studio on the subject, the majority of faculty there viewed the topic as inappropriate. And thus the profession perpetuates its marginalization.

The idea of using television as a real problem-solving format was a good one. It worked better than anyone could have imagined. People responded to it naturally and welcomed the opportunity to view architects as accessible leaders. The biggest obstacle to widespread use of television in design is the straight-laced self-image architects seem to have of themselves. For its part, the public is hungry for substantive television. Here's hoping they get it from architects in the future.

10

11

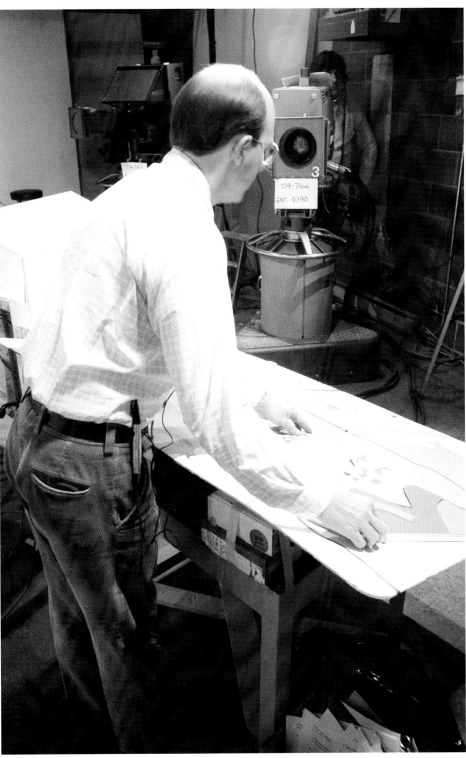

10   Chad Floyd hooks up with callers on the air. Many in the Watkins Glen shows (1980) were concerned about development of the Seneca Lake waterfront.

11   Ideas from callers at the 1980 Watkins Glen show are posted on pads around the studio.

12   After idea collection in the early shows, we present two-dimensional options to the community. Showing options upside down and talking to the camera at the same time is a bit daunting (Watkins Glen, 1980).

12

13   For the third show in Roanoke (1978), we published a questionnaire in the local newspaper asking viewers to mail in their preferences; hundreds were returned.

14   The shows appear to be spontaneous, but shots are scripted ahead of time by producer Floyd and are taped to each camera (Roanoke, 1979).

15   By the end of the final show in Roanoke (1979), the plan is unveiled, and an air of celebration ensues.

13

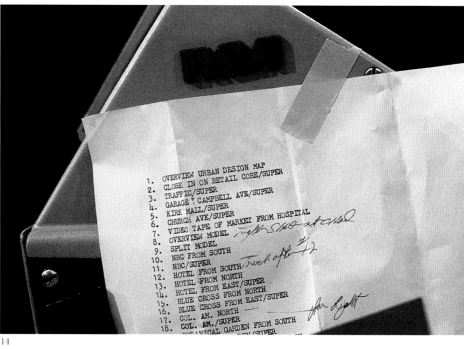

14

15

Chapter 21 Simplicity

Jim Childress

I wrote Bill Gates a letter with a two-word message, "Please simplify!" Needless to say, I never received a reply, but it felt good to complain. The computer world is over-complicated, with more and more layers of bells and whistles substituted for good useful design. I suspect that I am not alone in this feeling of over-abundance and over-complication.

I have always been enthusiastic about simple things, especially in architecture. Growing up in cattle country, south of Denver, Colorado, I developed an appreciation for simple landscapes and buildings. Sadly, that landscape today is as cluttered as the brain of the PC I am typing into.

As part of the Rhode Island School of Design's European Honors Program, I spent a year in Rome in 1977–78. I still rely on the simple diagrams of buildings that I studied during that experience. I discovered that the use of one material and one color in a building let the sunlight perform its magic and had a more enriching aesthetic quality than an endless variety of colors and textures (such as the post-modern buildings being built here in America at the time). The visual clutter of the old city was overwhelming, and I found myself increasingly taking trips to EUR, Mussolini's third Rome, to enjoy the open space and simple forms of the architecture there. Unaware, at the time, of the dark political origins of this part of the city, I found it calm and inviting, rather than domineering.

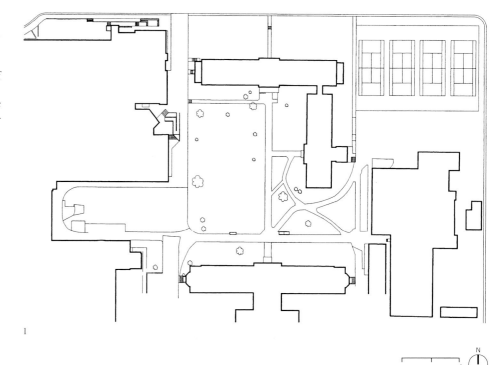

1

1   Plan of the existing jumble of buildings at the site for the new Campus Center at the University of Colorado Health Sciences Center.

2   The restrained use of materials and ornament reflect the original University of Colorado campus in Boulder, as well as the plea to "not overdo it", which has become so much a part of life in the Rocky Mountain West.

3   In designing the Campus Center, we needed to provide a calm haven in the middle of an otherwise chaotic urban campus.

2

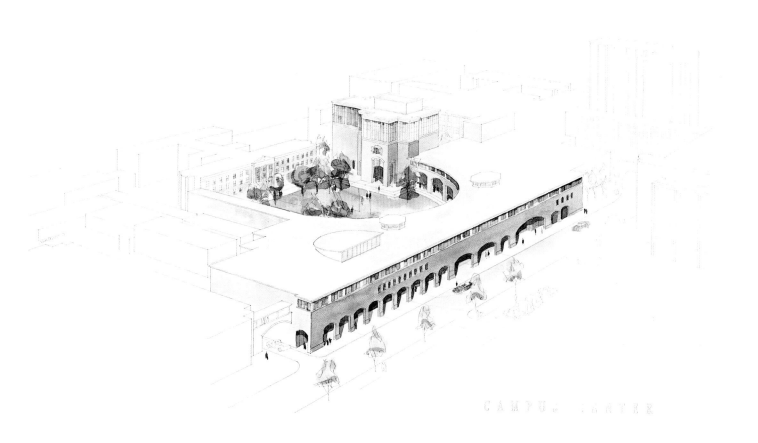

3

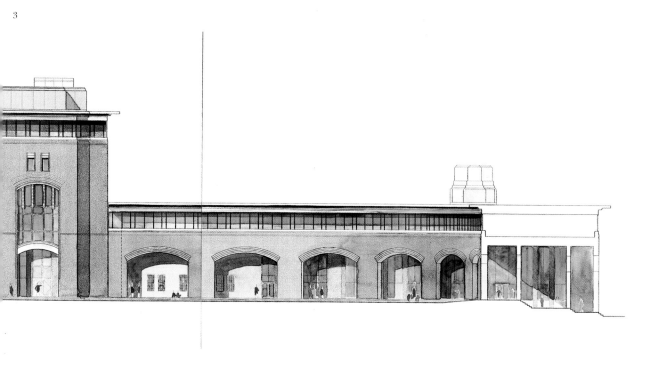

When I returned to work in the United States, a friend lured me to Centerbrook. I was excited about working with Charles Moore and his office, because he was brilliant and so well known. Although the quip "Moore is more" didn't suggest simplicity to me, what I found here, with those who would eventually become my partners, was a common appreciation for the Yankee mind-set. The partners had an appreciation for buildings that are intimate in scale (Connecticut is one-eighth the size of Colorado), accessible and inviting to many people (Connecticut has eight times as many people per square mile as Colorado), and have a sense of being inevitable. I found a shared appreciation for mill buildings and the tobacco barns along the Connecticut River. These are buildings designed for function and durability. They reflect the common sense of their builders.

I am always looking for inspiration from buildings that appear to be inevitable and that display common sense. I am drawn to Roche Dinkeloo's Creative Arts Center at Wesleyan University in nearby Middletown, Connecticut. A simple collection of limestone boxes, beautifully assembled, they create an inviting mini-campus. The architecture recedes into the background of the natural setting and acts as a backdrop to the colorful and active movement of students. The result is that the art created by students becomes as important as the architecture.

The Davis Museum and Cultural Center at Wellesley College in Massachusetts, by Rafael Moneo, is my favorite recent example of simple architecture in New England. I am curious to know whether he started with a simple idea and then carefully, perhaps hesitantly, added the complexities required by the program. Or, did he start with all the complexities of the program fully in mind, gradually editing them to the essence required to achieve the most with the least? Either way, the result is a simple brick box that

4

5

4   The Davis Museum and Cultural Center at Wellesley College by Rafael Moneo exhibits New England simplicity and common sense.

5   Roche Dinkeloo's Creative Arts Center at Wesleyan University has an understated straightforwardness that allows the art to flourish.

6   The side entry into our Neuroscience Center at Cold Spring Harbor Laboratory is restrained in its use of materials and openings. It relies on texture and proportion for interest.

6

turns every constraint of the site and program into a virtue. The unfolding interior spaces feel so simple and inevitable, yet they have enough variety to display a wide range of art. The progression of spaces from the entry up to the top floor climaxes in a sun-filled gallery located under a modern version of a mill building's sawtooth roof. Moneo is from Spain, yet he perfectly captured the New England imagery and spareness. He shows us that you don't have to be from a place to really understand it. You simply need to be a good architect.

A frequent cause of over-complication in a building's design is the desire to over-program. With good intentions, we often try to accommodate every need we can imagine, by creating a room or a space for it. The result can be a building that is so specific to a set of given needs that it will be very difficult to adapt it for future generations. In order for a building to accommodate the future, its plan, shell, and structural system need to be simple and open. One solution to "over-programming" is to build portions of a building in ways that can be easily changed.

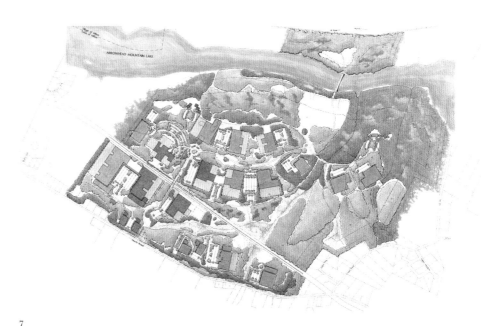

7

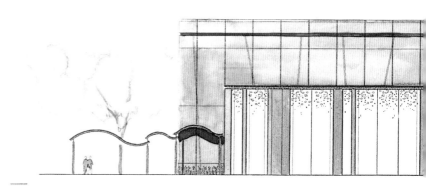

8

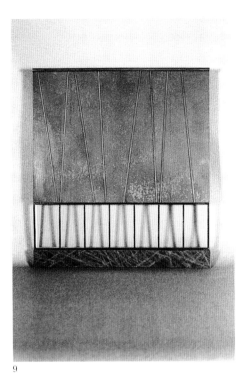

9

10

7 Planning for the Corporate and Manufacturing Campus, a new industrial complex in New England, envisions simple, generic buildings set into the woods. The overall plan organizes offices around a central spine of green space.

8 The manufacturing and office elevations are "camouflaged" to fit into the surrounding woods.

9 The manufacturing buildings are made of precast concrete with green slate aggregate. Lines of green slate mimic trees bending in the wind, and an embossing of grass-like texture provides a visual connection to the ground. Windows in the manufacturing area provide continuous views to the surrounding woods.

10 The offices look into the forest with the trees providing shading. The buildings are made of random vertical panels of clear glass and green slate "tree trunks". A frit pattern of leaves at the top provides shading until the new growth forest grows taller.

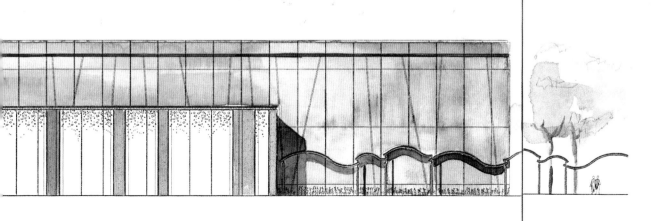

In order to make simple buildings, you need to include a process of editing. My partner Bill Grover regularly admonishes all of us, "Don't use every idea you ever had in one project." I have found that if I heed the critiques of my designs, especially from non-architects, I often arrive at solutions that have a feeling of being inevitable and that make good sense.

A budget cut can force simplicity as well. There are times when architects become so absorbed in the details of a project that they are unable to see how complicated the design has become. It is then that you need a friend like my collaborator, Hugh Brown, who is able to politely critique a design with a simple look that says, "That treasured artistic solution to a design problem is over-complicated, will probably leak, and cost a lot of money. Maybe you should find some inspiration in common sense."

11

12

13

14

15

11   Built to be competitive with local speculative office buildings, the Diebolt Building is constructed of simple concrete block, exposed steel, and a flat roof. The office block opens into the natural setting. Light is admitted to the warehouse by substituting glass block for the solid concrete block.

12   Shading is provided by the overhanging roof deck which is left exposed and is held down by galvanized steel straps.

13   A double banding of standard vinyl base, good quality indirect lighting, and inexpensive punched metal panels are all that are needed to create an inviting workday environment.

14   Placing the offices in the treetops made an otherwise generic office workplace enjoyable.

15&16   An addition to an existing house in Mystic, Connecticut relies simply on proportion and color to be successful and inviting.

16

17 For the City House on the East Coast, a new
    door with sidelight and canopy compose a
    simple abstraction of traditional entries.

18 Light fixtures have standard bare bulbs with
    shades of translucent plastic, using elementary
    school technology to interlock the pieces.

19 A new, stainless steel "rail" attached to a
    standard railroad bridge is designed to provide
    an economical yet elegant front door to
    downtown Worcester, Massachusetts.

17

18

19

Chapter 22 **Sticks**

Mark Simon

Most cultures have used ornament, but the Modern movement questioned its validity. We believe that ornament still plays an important role in revealing architectural forms, reinforcing the identity of places, and stimulating a response to architecture. How do we make it appropriate for our era?

One way to introduce ornament, without being literally historical, is to assemble simple sticks or stick-like elements to create patterns in lights, brackets, cornices, ceilings, and railings. We have applied and bent them in different ways to celebrate or distinguish their particular locations.

Ornament became an issue for the Modernists when Adolf Loos and some of his contemporaries declared it dead and erased it from their work (notwithstanding the brilliant ornament of other early Modernists such as Sullivan, Wright, and Mackintosh). Ornament returned with post-Modernism, but quickly deteriorated into stale pastiche and stuck-on clichés, called by one wag "the stuff that falls off buildings in an earthquake." Now ornament is again ebbing.

Buildings that are too clean tend toward sterility. Buildings should shelter psyches as well as bodies. People need to recognize who and where they are. They do this by establishing how each place is different from all others. The first Modern buildings were extraordinary and exhilarating, but their multiplication deadened souls. The International style was everywhere, and therefore nowhere special.

Ornament adds to the "somewhere" of a place. It offers richness in shadow, awakening us to light. It offers scale by which we measure. It makes us feel big by being small. It integrates the handmade into buildings, pointing out that someone, not something, has made the place. It serves as a visual trope, offering simile and metaphor for fun or understanding. It tells stories, evokes feelings. It surprises and delights.

Another task of ornament is to mediate the edges of buildings. In nature we rarely see the clean break between objects that we see in Modern architecture. Trees have roots and branches that tie them to the earth and sky. Occasionally, in Eastern cultures such as India, temples are carved from the "live" rock; there we see human-made mountains that are at once rooted and reach for the sky. In most of them, ornament weaves connections at their extremities.

Despite these benefits, ornament comes with a caveat; it will deaden if it is not fresh. So we have explored how ornament might express our own times.

One option comes from a handy misreading of Modernists who preached that buildings should show how they were made. (This is not easy; in fact, it is usually costly. We architects have almost all heard that Mies's Seagram building "expresses" its construction with I-beams that are not truly structural, but that are essentially ornament applied to the exterior.) We are still very much a mechanical society. Perhaps ornament can stand in and show how it was made, with less effort than the entire building. Perhaps ornament can express the putting together of things, the making of itself.

Remembering that we are also an electrical society, perhaps the ornament should occasionally plug in and light up.

1   The McKim House living room frieze is made of simple sticks, glued to the wall. This lowers the apparent height of a vertical space.

2   A Bauhaus light fixture of sticks. Irmgard Sörenson-Popitz, Suspended Construction, 1924.

3   Like so many others, this Bauhaus chair is made of planes and sticks. Gerrit Rietveld, Highback Chair, 1919.

1

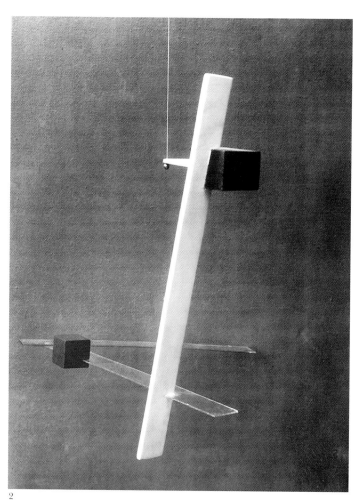

2

3

Or perhaps it can also express the mass production of things by being made of repetitive elements—simple elements for our efficient times. John Lennon said that he idolized Chuck Berry because Berry's best songs used almost only one note. That appeals, using only one note. If ornament can have a limited variety of parts (or notes), that might do.

Hence, our exploration of sticks as ornament.

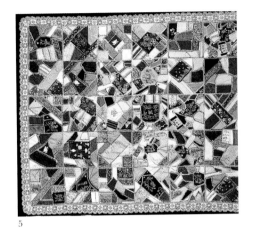
5

6

4

7

8

4   The McKim House porch railing sticks mimic early American "crazy quilts,"
    Chinese grilles, and Adirondack Camp architecture.
5   An American crazy quilt.
6   A Chinese grille in a garden wall in Suzhou.
7   Even fireplace stone can be treated like sticks in a board-and-batten pattern,
    as found in the Pond House.
8   The Marsh Estate roofs are held up by trees that turn into lumber.
9   Thin sticks curve easily atop the Pond House trellis.

9

10   The McKim House dining table legs and roof brackets are also collages of sticks.
11   The eagles at the Marsh Estate's entry sit on a nest of lumber.

11

12

13

14

15

12 This small library in the Simon-Bellamy House I has rectangular bicycle reflectors laid in ornate patterns to make a plastic "fireworks".

13 The Simon-Bellamy House I hallway is topped with floating stick trim that hides lighting.

14 The twisted balusters of the Bernstein House's railing offer just the right amount of pattern and ornament.

15 The pool of the Bernstein House is sheltered by a carefully wrought, wooden trellis of interwoven sticks that cast changing geometric shadows.

16 Neon sticks light up our renovation of a dark basement space at MIT's Media Lab.

17 At the Simon-Bellamy House II, lights in aluminum stick/trays make a rug pattern on the living room ceiling, while simulataneously giving the impression of a modern sculpture.

16

17

18

19

18 The nautically inspired, wriggling balusters at
    Nauticus.
19 Standard linear fixtures animate the Brandeis
    Shapiro Center conference room in a
    recollection of de Stijl.
20 An eye of sticks centers the oval entry rotunda
    at the Centennial Building, a classroom and
    studio building at Pomfret School.
21 The walls and ceiling surrounding the Guyott
    pool table dance with mahogany sticks. They
    recall boat houses and oars, appropriate here
    on the shore.

20

21

Hardware stores are great places from which to get ideas. Look at all the design decisions that had to be made in order to get all those gadgets and devices on the market! Every single one required some thought about function, dimension, appearance, materials, and the cost to manufacture, distribute, and market. There are lots of great materials and objects that can be used in architecture for purposes other than those for which they were intended.

2

3

1

1   A light fixture made of plastic sockets plugged into one another.
2   Salad bowls were used to make the column capitals in the living room of the Riley House II.
3   A "hardware store technology" light fixture made from bent steel conduit, junction boxes, and utility light globes.
4   The cornice motif at the Ed McMahon Mass Communications Center at Quinnipiac College utilizes radio station microphones.
5   A glare-reducing curtain is made of different-sized loose-leaf notebook rings at the Koizim House.
6   Stainless steel flue pipes make elegant columns at Neurogen IV.
7   Standard hardware cloth is used as a shimmering ceiling at Neurogen III.

4

5

6

7

Chapter 24 Success

Bill Grover

Every architect has his or her own personal definition of success.

Among the possibilities for its measurement are:

- Survival success:
  Am I staying alive while doing architecture?

- Financial success:
  How much time do I spend worrying about money?

- Success in the firm:
  Do I have time to participate in the design of my projects?

- Critical success:
  Do others like my projects?

- Design success:
  Am I pleased with the outcome of the project?

- Business success:
  How much time do I spend resolving business problems?

- Success with clients:
  Are they happy with my work? Will they return, or recommend me to others?

- Professional success:
  Do I have the respect of my peers and those with whom I work?

- Personal success:
  What percentage of my waking hours are spent doing things I enjoy?

The peril lies in placing too much emphasis on one measurement over another. If, for example, success means spreading one's self so thin that life cannot be enjoyed, or that the pleasure of design must be handed to others for lack of time, or that worrying about money becomes too important, the architectural life gets out of balance.

Here are some guidelines that have proved to be useful to us:

1. It is bad luck to turn down a job. Every job is an opportunity to design something. No project is too small or undeserving of design attention.

2. Art always comes first, money second (a *close* second—you cannot keep creating art if you have no money).

3. Do not be disappointed if a client rejects your design. It is another opportunity to design. There are many answers to the same problem.

4. Always try hard to exceed the client's expectations. This means establishing realistic expectations that you can exceed.

5. No matter what they may say, or what you might think, cost is foremost in the minds of all clients, regardless of how wealthy they may be. It is possible to exceed an unlimited budget. Make sure everyone has a clear, written understanding of the expected cost of the project. Have a plan for how you will proceed when it comes in over budget.

6. Meet with your partners, senior staff, office manager, and bookkeeper *every* Friday for a 1.5-hour lunch, in a private room in a nice restaurant away from the office. Follow an agenda. Review the finances and schedule each employee's time for the next week. If you have problems, sort them out once a week. Strictly limit the meeting to 1.5 hours. Everybody should get up and walk out when the time is up. If you do not, the meetings will become longer and longer over time, and nobody will want to waste their time on them.

7. Be as diverse and flexible as possible. Every architect should be able to do everything: write good letters, get jobs, design them, build models, take out the trash, charm clients, do construction drawings, do construction administration, respect everybody. Don't compartmentalize architecture. One exception: photography.

8. Have projects professionally photographed. Spend the money on the best professional architectural photographer you can find. Map out the views you want on a plan of the building. Go to the job site with the photographer. Explain what is most important to you about the building and what views best tell the story behind your design. It may seem expensive, but it will be the best money you ever spent.

9. Enter award programs, especially state, regional, and national AIA programs. Make the presentation simple and beautiful. Never, under any circumstances, include a bad photograph in any presentation, no matter how important you may think it is in explaining your concept. If at first you do not win an award, keep entering the project. The juries are always different. If it is a good building, some jury will recognize it.

10. Learn to recognize problems as opportunities to show how good you really are.

11. Bad news travels fast. An unhappy client will spread the word about you. Everyone in the world will know about it within a few days. A satisfied client will be a good friend and a good reference. Remember this when tempted to tell a client to go to hell.

12. You cannot please everybody, but it is most important to please your client and yourself.

13. If you focus on making every project an artistic success, you will get rich. If you give first priority to making money, you will go broke.

14. Clients are spending a lot of money on your services. They should enjoy themselves. You should, too.

As American architects we are proud of the fact that, although we are interested in tradition and can learn from it, we are not burdened by it. In fact, we are delighted by the notion of rejecting it, bending it, stretching it, and expanding it to fit. Mark Simon talks about how we use the "imagined past" as a source for our architectural inspiration, as opposed to actually copying. Charles Moore said, "creativity is not revealing your sources" (and he never revealed the source of that quote). Architectural forms evolve or mutate over the years as new materials become available, but also by accident because we do not look carefully at what was done before and we invent something new nearly every time we design a building.

Not reading the instruction book (or the history book) is an American custom that often gets us into trouble. Occasionally it also results in putting things together in an odd way that works. These accidental collisions often result in something interesting. If the result is successful, we are hailed as being clever. If it fails, we are regarded, perhaps, as adventurous for having tried something new or, more likely, branded as a failure or, worse yet, boring. It is clearly more interesting to try the adventurous route if one can afford the possibility of failure. Practicing with others can keep the adventurous spirit alive, especially if they provide the encouragement to take chances.

1   "Ballybung", the President's House, is inspired by the English Regency style and Sir John Soane's house in London, but it is not a copy of anything.

2   The grand porch of the President's House overlooks Long Island Sound. Note the column fluting, made of ordinary lumber and tapered to achieve entasis at minimal cost.

3   Why not have every chair different from every other one?

4&5 A grand central stair in the President's House, with mirrors and skylights, acts as a lantern to distribute light to the heart of the house.

3

4

5

Chapter 26 **Our Place**

Bill Grover, Jeff Riley, Mark Simon, Chad Floyd, and Jim Childress

Places accumulate character from those who design them, occupy them, and pass through them. The spirit and energy of those people seem to get into the place and remain with it. The best places are those that wear well and survive over many years, improving with occupancy, modification, and renovation.

In our wonderful office, an old manufacturing building in Centerbrook, Connecticut, we feel the presence and influence of those who worked and celebrated here with us and before us. Those people left visible and invisible traces of the past. Inspired by that, we strive for all of our buildings to become better and more endearing with age.

1

2

3

4

5

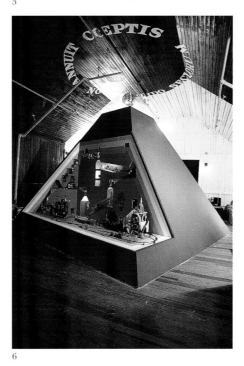
6

7

8

9

10

11

13

12

1 We once rented part of our building to The Yellow Daffodil store, seen to the left.

2 Our roof-top deck is adorned with flower gardens and a wisteria-ladened trellis, all tended to by our Manager of Finances, Carol Redfield.

3&4 Our building, called the Bit Shop, was full of machinery when we bought it in 1970. We have made some of that machinery into decoration and furniture.

5 Our first CAD machine, circa 1978.

6&7 The house that served as the Bit Shop's office was Charles Moore's home. After 1978, it became Centerbrook's "union hall" and venue for the annual ping-pong tournaments.

8&9 After the devastating flood of 1982, we rebuilt the lost buildings and harnessed the waterfall with a space-age turbine to produce our own electricity.

10 Nina Pae in our well-used wood-working shop.

11 The banner from our first television Design-a-thon in Dayton, Ohio hangs in our main stairway.

12 We floated an aluminum "paper airplane" into Centerbrook to keep the rain off.

13 The moose in the front office was given to us by a client.

14

15

16

17

18

19

20

21

22

23

25

24

26

27

14 The Bah Reliefs, starring Trip Wyeth on guitar,
    Whit Huber and Jeff Riley on violin, Jim
    Childress on clarinet, and Richard King on
    drums, play at the annual Christmas party, 1982.

15 The grounds of our factory make a perfect
    setting for large-scale celebrations.

16 The "Circus" party, one of many parties in which
    we ask the guests to participate in the
    entertainment.

17 The set for the "Wild West" party under
    construction.

18 Our reconstructed buildings, set on concrete
    piers, survive a second flood in 1990.

19 The office staff, circa 1975. From left to right:
    Charles Moore, Ginger Rutledge, Glenn
    Arbonies, Mary Ann Rumney, Mark Simon, Jeff
    Riley, Ron Eichorn, Bob Harper, and Bill Grover.

20 The women of Centerbrook at the "Academy
    Awards" party, 1998.

21 "The Pounding Fartner Quintet" at the
    "Academy Awards" party. From left to right: Jim
    Childress (clarinet), Mark Simon (vocal), Jeff
    Riley (piano), Chad Floyd (drums), and Bill
    Grover (trumpet).

22 The office staff, circa 1979, with partner Chad
    Floyd (far right) added, and newly hired Jim
    Childress (seated second from right).

23 The office staff, circa 1995, with principal Jim
    Coan (front row, second from left).

24 Bill Grover on the cornet.

25 Chad and Brenda Floyd at the AIA Firm Award
    party in San Francisco.

26 Mark (Captain Hook) Simon at the "Hawaiian
    Luau Pirate" party in our back yard by the river.

27 Every year, Jeff Riley appears as Father Christmas
    bearing gifts to the beat of Gladys Knight and the
    Pips.

William H. Grover, FAIA

Bill Grover studied mechanical engineering at Cornell University. He was awarded a Bachelor of Arts in Industrial Design from the Art Center College of Design in 1962. From 1962 to 1965 he worked as an industrial designer at the General Motors Technical Center. After obtaining a Master of Architecture from Yale in 1969, Mr. Grover began working for Charles Moore in New Haven, and in 1975 he and Moore formed a new firm, Moore Grover Harper, the predecessor firm to Centerbrook Architects.

In addition to undertaking more than 35 projects at Cold Spring Harbor Laboratory in New York, under the directorship of Nobel Laureate Dr. James D. Watson, Mr. Grover has been the architect for numerous private homes, college buildings, and research and teaching laboratories for academic and corporate clients such as IES, Neurogen, Alexion, Vion, Dekalb, and Philips Exeter Academy. In 1984, he was invested into the College of Fellows of the American Institute of Architects (AIA). In addition to architecture, Mr. Grover practices watercolor painting, sail boat racing, and playing jazz on the cornet.

Jefferson B. Riley, FAIA

Jeff Riley was awarded a Bachelor of Arts from Lawrence University in Appleton, Wisconsin in 1968 and a Master of Architecture from Yale University in 1972.

In 1975, he was a founding partner of Moore Grover Harper, which later became Centerbrook Architects. In addition to numerous houses, community centers, churches, museums, and educational facilities throughout the United States, since 1979 Mr. Riley has been the architect for more than 25 projects at Quinnipiac College in Hamden, Connecticut. Early in his career he studied the art of wooden boat building and began touring and photographing villages around the world. Both interests have informed his architectural designs ever since. Since 1990, Mr. Riley has also worked with the United Church of Christ Fellowship of Architects to develop liturgical design guidelines. In 1992, he was invested into the College of Fellows of the AIA, and in 1999 he received the Lucia R. Briggs Distinguished Achievement Award from his alma mater, Lawrence University.

Mark Simon, FAIA

Mark Simon was awarded a Bachelor of Arts, cum laude, with honors in sculpture in 1968 from Brandeis University and a Master of Architecture from Yale University in 1972.

The son of sculptor Sidney Simon, he learned about wood and design at an early age. Mr. Simon developed his own sculptural skills at Brandeis and, after graduation from Yale, he worked as a cabinetmaker, developing a concern for architectural detail. In 1978, he became a partner in Moore Grover Harper, now Centerbrook Architects. In 1986, Mr. Simon served as Chair of the AIA Committee on Design. In 1990, he was advanced to the AIA College of Fellows. Though still enjoying residential projects, his practice includes larger work, notably Nauticus—the National Maritime Center in Norfolk, Virginia; the University of Connecticut School of Business; the Nortel Networks Executive Briefing Center in North Carolina; the Yale Child Study Center in New Haven; and a Film and Visitors Center at the University of Nebraska in Lincoln.

Chad Floyd, FAIA

Chad Floyd was awarded both his undergraduate degrees in drama and English and his Master of Architecture from Yale University in 1966 and 1973, respectively. He was awarded the Winchester Traveling Fellowship from Yale in 1973 and traveled in India. Before joining Centerbrook as a partner in 1978, he spent two years on a National Endowment for the Arts Grant, researching the role of architecture in public celebration.

Mr. Floyd pioneered the use of live Design-a-Thon television programming as an urban design technique, with projects in Dayton, Ohio; Springfield, Massachusetts; Roanoke, Virginia; and Watkins Glen, New York. Mr. Floyd's other special interests have included theaters and art museums, with projects such as the Hood Museum of Art at Dartmouth College, the Norton Art Museum in West Palm Beach, and the Garde Theater in New London, Connecticut. In addition, Mr. Floyd has designed numerous other projects for both Dartmouth College and Pfizer Corporation. In 1991, he was advanced to the AIA College of Fellows.

James Cabell Childress, AIA

Jim Childress was awarded a Bachelor of Fine Arts and a Bachelor of Architecture from the Rhode Island School of Design in 1977 and 1978, respectively. He joined Centerbrook in 1979, becoming a partner in 1996.

Mr. Childress's work includes numerous projects at Cold Spring Harbor Laboratory in New York. In addition, he has been the architect for the Heckscher Museum of Art in Huntington, New York; the expansion of the Trudeau Institute, a national center for immunology research in Saranac Lake, New York; the Campus Center for the University of Colorado Health Sciences Center in Denver; the headquarters for the National Outdoor Leadership School in Lander, Wyoming; a new campus for the Hamden Hall Country Day School in Hamden, Connecticut; and a master plan and buildings for Briarwood College in Southington, Connecticut. He has also designed more than 20 single family houses. He was recently selected by *Interior Magazine* as one of the past decade's "40 National Architects under 40".

John Morris Dixon, FAIA

Recipient of a Bachelor of Architecture from M.I.T. in 1955, John Dixon spent two years as an apprentice architect before entering a long-term career in architectural journalism. He held staff positions at *Progressive Architecture* and at *Architectural Forum* before serving as editor-in-chief of *Progressive Architecture* from 1972 to 1996.

In 1977, Mr. Dixon was named a Fellow of the AIA, and in 1983 he chaired the Institute's Committee on Design, on which he remains active. He has lectured widely and has served on numerous awards juries, as well as design competition juries for such projects as the Astronauts Memorial at Cape Canaveral and the Evanston, Illinois, public library. He has been appointed a peer reviewer in the Federal General Services Administration's Design Excellence program. Mr. Dixon is now a freelance writer and consultant on architecture, as well as associate editor of *Architectural Research Quarterly*. In recent times, he has had articles published in *Architectural Record, Competitions, Domus, Harvard Design Magazine, House & Garden,* and *Residential Architect.*

Project Credits

Apartment in New York
New York, New York, 1989
Project Designer: Mark Simon
Project Team: Roger U. Williams (project
manager)

Baldwin House
Essex, Connecticut, 1985
Client: Dr. Robert Baldwin
Project Designer: William H. Grover
Project Team: Leonard J. Wyeth (project
manager)

Bernstein House
East Hampton, New York, 1999
Client: Jon and Penny Bernstein
Project Designer: Mark Simon
Project Team: Margaret H. Lyons (project
manager), Jennifer Lewis

**Brandeis University, Carl and Ruth Shapiro
Admissions Center**
Waltham, Massachusetts, 1994
Client: Brandeis University
Project Designers: Mark Simon and Mahdad
Saniee
Project Team: Michelle R. LaFoe, Sheryl A.
Milardo, Darin C. Cook, Elizabeth A.
DiSalvo, John M. Doyle

Burns House
Santa Monica, California, 1974
Client: Lee Burns
Project Designers: Charles W. Moore with
Richard Chylinski

Cape Cod Cottage
Eastham, Massachusetts, 1984
Project Designer: Chad Floyd
Project Team: J. Whitney Huber (project
manager)

Cedar Rapids Museum of Art
Cedar Rapids, Iowa, 1989
Client: Cedar Rapids Museum of Art
Project Designers: Glenn W. Arbonies and
Richard L. King with Charles W. Moore
consulting
Project Team: Mahdad Saniee

Central Lakes College
Brainerd, Minnesota, 1996
Client: Central Lakes College
Project Designers: Chad Floyd with Stephen
B. Holmes
Project Team: Jonathan G. Parks (job
captain), Susan E. Wyeth
Prime Architect: Symmes, Maini and McKee
Associates/Winsor Faricy: Richard Faricy
(project executive), James Cox
(principal), Mark Beckman (project
architect), Steve Sanneman, (construction
administration)

**Cheshire Academy, John J. White '38 Science
and Technology Building**
Cheshire, Connecticut, 1998
Client: Cheshire Academy
Project Designers: Mark Simon with Steven
E. Tiezzi
Project Team: Dennis J. Dowd, Jeffrey Gotta,
C. Todd Delfosse, Julia W. Harrison

City House
East Coast, United States, 1998
Project Designer: James C. Childress
Project Team: Lucy Ciletti (project
manager), Padraic H. Ryan, Michael R.
Stoddard

Colby College, Student Center
Waterville, Maine, 1986
Client: Colby College
Project Designer: Jefferson B. Riley
Project Team: J. Whitney Huber (project
manager), D. Randy Wilmot, Jennifer
Tate, Sandra Vlock, Robert Coolidge,
Roger U. Williams, Glenn W. Arbonies,
Elaine Larry, David Hajian, Charles
Balfour

Cold Spring Harbor Laboratory, Airslie House
Cold Spring Harbor, New York, 1974
Client: Cold Spring Harbor Laboratory
Project Designers: William H. Grover and
Charles W. Moore
Project Team: Richard B. Oliver

**Cold Spring Harbor Laboratory, Ballybung
(President's House)**
Cold Spring Harbor, New York, 1994
Client: Cold Spring Harbor Laboratory
Project Designers: William H. Grover and
Mahdad Saniee
Project Team: Paul L. Shainberg, George
W. Penniman

**Cold Spring Harbor Laboratory, David and
Fanny Luke Building**
Cold Spring Harbor, New York, 1999
Client: Cold Spring Harbor Laboratory
Project Designers: James C. Childress
Project Team: Lucy Ciletti (project
manager)

**Cold Spring Harbor Laboratory, Grace
Auditorium**
Cold Spring Harbor, New York, 1986
Client: Cold Spring Harbor Laboratory
Project Designers: William H. Grover with
Charles W. Moore
Project Team: James C. Childress

**Cold Spring Harbor Laboratory, Jones
Laboratory**
Cold Spring Harbor, New York, 1976
Client: Cold Spring Harbor Laboratory
Project Designers: William H. Grover and
Charles W. Moore
Project Team: Ronald Eichorn

**Cold Spring Harbor Laboratory, McClintock
Laboratory**
Cold Spring Harbor, New York, 1993
Client: Cold Spring Harbor Laboratory
Project Designers: William H. Grover and
Nick Deaver
Project Team: Susan E. Wyeth

**Cold Spring Harbor Laboratory, Neuroscience
Center**
Cold Spring Harbor, New York, 1991
Client: Cold Spring Harbor Laboratory
Project Designers: William H. Grover and
James C. Childress, with Charles W.
Moore (consulting on conceptual design)

Project Team: Daniel H. Glynn, Jon M.
Lavy, Susan E. Wyeth, Kathleen Amrock,
Michael J. Milne, Michael J. Crosbie,
Sheryl A. Milardo, John D. Kennedy

**Cold Spring Harbor Laboratory, Waste Water
Treatment Plant**
Cold Spring Harbor, New York, 1976
Client: Cold Spring Harbor Laboratory
Project Designers: William H. Grover and
Robert L. Harper, with Charles W. Moore

Colgate University, Art and Art History Building
Hamilton, New York, 2000
Client: Colgate University
Project Designers: Chad Floyd with Susan E.
Wyeth
Project Team: E. Russell Learned (job
captain), Charles G. Mueller, Jennifer
Lewis, Mark Herter, Reno J. Migani Jr.,
Ted Tolis

Connecticut River House
Essex, Connecticut, 1987
Project Designers: Jefferson B. Riley with
Leonard J. Wyeth

Corporate and Manufacturing Campus
New England, 1998, Project
Project Designers: James C. Childress and
James A. Coan
Project Team: Margaret H. Lyons, Lucy
Ciletti, Padraic H. Ryan
Associated Architects: Dunn Associates:
Christopher W. Dunn, Mark Hamelin;
Guillot-Vivian-Viehmann Architects, Inc.:
Douglas R. Viehmann, Ann Vivian

Crowell Studio
Long Island, New York, 1984
Client: David and Joan Crowell
Project Designer: Mark Simon
Project Team: Leonard J. Wyeth (project
manager)

**Dartmouth College, Amos Tuck School of
Business Administration**
Hanover, New Hampshire, 1994
Client: Dartmouth College
Project Designers: Chad Floyd and Susan E.
Wyeth
Byrne Hall Project Team: D. Michael
Hellinghausen (project manager),
Charles G. Mueller, Sheryl A. Milardo,
Robert G. Proctor, Craig W. Grund,
Michael J. Crosbie
Stell Hall Project Team: D. Michael
Hellinghausen (project manager),
Charles G. Mueller, Sheryl A. Milardo

Dartmouth College, Hood Museum of Art
Hanover, New Hampshire, 1985
Client: Dartmouth College
Project Designers: Chad Floyd and Charles
W. Moore
Project Team: Glenn W. Arbonies (project
manager), Richard L. King, James C.
Childress, James A. Coan, James R.
Martin, Stephen L. Lloyd, Leonard J.
Wyeth, Julie H. Miner, Beth Rubenstein,
Jennifer Tate

Dartmouth College, Wilson Hall
Hanover, New Hampshire, 1984
Client: Dartmouth College
Project Designer: Chad Floyd
Project Team: Richard L. King (project manager), Steven L. Lloyd, Julie H. Miner

Dayton Riverdesign Master Plan
Dayton, Ohio, 1976
Client: Miami River Conservancy
Project Designers: Chad Floyd and Charles W. Moore
Project Team: Jefferson B. Riley, William H. Grover, Robert L. Harper
Associated Architects: Lorenz and Williams

Dayton Riverlanding
Dayton, Ohio, 1978
Client: Miami River Conservancy
Project Designers: Chad Floyd and Jefferson B. Riley with Charles W. Moore
Associated Architects: Lorenz and Williams

Dekalb Plant Genetics Discovery Research Center
Stonington, Connecticut, 1992
Client: Dekalb Plant Genetics Corporation
Project Designers: William H. Grover and Sheri Bryant Lucero
Project Team: Ida Vorum, Robert L. Harper, Roger U. Williams, Susan E. Wyeth, Michael J. Milne, Sheryl A. Milardo, Michael J. Crosbie, C. Todd Delfosse, Daniel H. Glynn, Walker J. Burns III, Jonathan G. Parks, D. Michael Hellinghausen, Jean E. Smajstrla, Matthew C. Conley, Michael Garner, Daniel M. Vickers, Stephen B. Holmes, George W. Penniman

Diebolt & Company Office and Manufacturing Buildings
Old Lyme, Connecticut, 1998
Client: Diebolt & Company
Project Designer: James C. Childress
Project Team: Stephen B. Holmes (project manager), Susan E. Wyeth, Jeffrey Gotta

East Hampton Library and Community Center
East Hampton, Connecticut, 1986
Client: Town of East Hampton
Project Designer: Mark Simon
Project Team: Stephen L. Lloyd (project manager), Walker J. Burns III, Jennifer Tate

East Lyme Library and Community Center
East Lyme, Connecticut, 1990
Client: Town of East Lyme
Project Designer: Mark Simon
Project Team: Leonard J. Wyeth (project manager), Jean E. Smajstrla (job captain), Daniel H. Glynn, Michael J. Crosbie, Jonathan G. Parks, William Egan, Robert Coolidge, Thomas Morton, Michael Casolo, John Barteck, Sheryl A. Milardo

Eisenstein House
Midwest, 1993
Client: Edward Eisenstein
Project Designers: Mark Simon and Charles G. Mueller
Project Team: C. Todd Delfosse

Elliott House
Ligonier, Pennsylvania, 1983
Client: Ann Elliott and Peter Gruen
Project Designer: Jefferson B. Riley
Project Team: Julie H. Miner (project manager)

Elmwood Park
Roanoke, Virginia, 1982
Client: City of Roanoke, Virginia
Project Designer: Chad Floyd
Project Team: James A. Coan (project manager)

Erle House
Guilford, Connecticut, 1994
Client: Ms. Syoko Aki Erle
Project Designers: James C. Childress
Project Team: Paul L. Shainberg (project manager), Christopher Arelt, Matthew Johnson

Guyott House
Connecticut Coast, 1995
Client: Mr. and Mrs. Francis R. Guyott, Jr.
Project Designers: Mark Simon with Dennis J. Dowd
Project Team: Steven E. Tiezzi, Darin C. Cook, Paul L. Shainberg, Elizabeth A. DiSalvo, Mahdad Saniee, Sheryl A. Milardo, Robert L. Harper, Megan N. Gibson, Edward J. Keagle

Hamden Hall Country Day School, Master Plan
Hamden, Connecticut, 1998
Client: Hamden Hall Country Day School
Project Designers: James C. Childress and Steven E. Tiezzi
Associated Architect: The Kagan Company: Rosemary Benivegna

Heckscher Museum of Art
Huntington, New York, In Design
Client: Heckscher Museum of Art
Project Designers: William H. Grover and James C. Childress
Project Team: Steven E. Tiezzi (project manager), Jeffrey Gotta, Matthew C. Conley, Sheri Bryant Lucero, Christopher Arelt, Julia W. Harrison

House in Connecticut
Greenwich, Connecticut, 1990
Project Designer: Chad Floyd
Project Team: Roger U. Williams (project manager), Sheri Bryant Lucero, James A. Coan, Robert Coolidge, Jonathan G. Parks, Matt Malakias, Michael A. P. Casolo

House on the Connecticut Seashore
Connecticut, 1989
Project Designers: Chad Floyd and Susan E. Wyeth
Project Team: Howard Langer, Steve Dadajian, Jonathan G. Parks, Matt Malakias

House in the Country
Connecticut, 1991
Project Designer: Chad Floyd
Project Team: Nick Deaver and Kevin Henson (project managers); Sheri Bryant Lucero

House in the Hudson Valley
Upstate New York, 1994
Project Designers: Jefferson B. Riley with Charles G. Mueller
Project Team: Steven E. Tiezzi, Robert G. Proctor, John M. Doyle, J. Richard Staub, Sheryl A. Milardo

House in Killingworth
Connecticut, 1992
Project Designers: William H. Grover and Nick Deaver
Project Team: Michael Garner

House near New York
New York Suburbs, 1976
Project Designers: Charles W. Moore and Richard B. Oliver

House in Mystic, Connecticut
Mystic, Connecticut, 1998
Project Designer: James C. Childress
Project Team: Mark Herter (project manager), Thomas Salmaso

House in Southern Connecticut
Connecticut, 1996
Project Designer: William H. Grover
Project Team: Charlotte C. Breed (project manager), Sheryl A. Milardo

House near Washington, DC
Suburb of Washington, DC, 1982
Project Designers: Charles W. Moore and Mark Simon with James C. Childress

Kaplan House
Chester, Connecticut, 1984
Client: Howard and Jill Kaplan
Project Designer: William H. Grover
Project Team: Stephen L. Lloyd (project manager)

Koizim House
Westport, Connecticut, 1970
Client: Harvey L. Koizim
Project Designers: Charles W. Moore, Arthur Ballman
Project Team: William H. Grover

Lawrence University, Wriston Art Center
Appleton, Wisconsin, 1989
Client: Lawrence University
Project Designer: Jefferson B. Riley
Project Team: D. Michael Hellinghausen (project manager), Walker J. Burns III, David Hajian, Charles G. Mueller, James R. Martin, Jon M. Lavy, Jonathan G. Parks, Michael J. Milne, James A. Coan, Sheryl A. Milardo, Stacia Hazard

Lego Imagination Center at Walt Disney World
Orlando, Florida, 1977
Client: Lego Systems Inc.
Project Designers: Centerbrook Architects and Planners with Lego Systems Inc.
Centerbrook Design Team: Mark Simon with Steven E. Tiezzi
Centerbrook Project Team: Margaret H. Lyons
Lego Project Team: William Higgins, Vince Rubino, Marc Marano, Francie Berger, Lori Garcia

Library in New York City
New York, New York, 1985
Project Designer: Mark Simon
Project Team: Leonard J. Wyeth (project
manager)

Long View
New England, 1991
Project Designers: Mark Simon with
Matthew C. Conley
Project Team: D. Michael Hellinghausen,
Jean E. Smajstrla, Jon M. Lavy, Charles G.
Mueller, Dennis J. Dowd, Sheryl A.
Milardo, Michael J. Milne, Kevin Henson,
Robert G. Proctor, William Egan, Howard
A. Langner, Rossana Santos, Howard
Rosenberg, Michael Casolo, Robert Stein,
David Altman

Marsh Estate
East Coast, United States, 1991
Project Designers: Mark Simon with
Mahdad Saniee
Project Team: William H. Grover, Sheri
Bryant Lucero, C. Todd Delfosse,
Jonathan G. Parks, Ann Patterson, Jean E.
Smajstrla, Evan P. Markiewicz, Howard A.
Langner, Robert Coolidge, Wanmaizan
Wanradzi, Robert L. Harper, Glenn W.
Arbonies, Kathleen Amrock, Michael A.
P. Casolo, James C. Childress, Matthew C.
Conley, Carol Curren, Michael J. Crosbie,
Dennis J. Dowd, Susan E. Wyeth, William
Egan, Daniel H. Glynn, Stacia Hazard,
Kevin Henson, Vincent Jordan, John D.
Kennedy, Richard L. King, Jon M. Lavy,
Mimi Locher, James R. Martin, Sheryl A.
Milardo, Michael J. Milne, Robert G.
Proctor, Howard Rosenberg, Paul L.
Shainberg, Steven E. Tiezzi, Chris Todd,
D. Randy Wilmot, Leonard J. Wyeth

Martha's Vineyard House
Martha's Vineyard, Massachusetts, 1997
Project Designer: Mark Simon
Project Team: Mahdad Saniee, Paul L.
Shainberg, and Jon M. Lavy (project
managers); Michael Garner, Christopher
Foster, Jonas M. Goldberg

**Massachusetts Institute of Technology, Media
Laboratory**
Cambridge, Massachusetts, 1994
Client: Massachusetts Institute of
Technology
Project Designers: Mark Simon with
Mahdad Saniee
Project Team: Peter T. Coffin, D. Michael
Hellinghausen, Darin C. Cook, Sheryl A.
Milardo, Stephen B. Holmes, Megan N.
Gibson, Julia W. Harrison, C. Todd
Delfosse, Walker J. Burns III, Paul L.
Shainberg, Elizabeth A. DiSalvo

McKim House
Fishers Island, New York, 1988
Client: Charlotte McKim
Project Designers: Mark Simon and
Leonard J. Wyeth

Miller House
The Berkshires, 1991
Project Designer: William H. Grover
Project Team: Sheri Bryant Lucero (project
manager), Walker J. Burns III

Minnesota History Center
St. Paul, Minnesota, 1984, Project
Client: Minnesota Historical Society
Project Designers: Charles W. Moore, James
C. Childress, William H. Grover
Project Team: John Blood
Associated Architects: Winsor-Faricy

**National Outdoor Leadership School,
Headquarters**
Lander, Wyoming, 2001
Client: National Outdoor Leadership
School
Project Designer: James C. Childress
Project Team: Thomas J. Lodge (project
manager), Jeffrey Gotta, Peggy V.
Sullivan, Anita Macagno Cecchetto, Susan
J. Pinckney, Wendy B. Johnson, Lucy
Ciletti

Nauticus, The National Maritime Center
Norfolk, Virginia, 1994
Client: The National Maritime Center
Authority
Project Designers: Mark Simon and James
A. Coan
Project Team: Charles W. Moore, Chad
Floyd, James R. Martin, Jonathan G.
Parks, Wanmaizan Wanradzi, C. Todd
Delfosse, Kyra Hauser
Associated Architects: Shriver & Holland
Associates: Henry V. Shriver, (partner-in-
charge), Aubrey C. Brock (project
architect), Joseph T. Gaber, Joseph C.
Freeman, Timothy J. Bell, John W. Myers,
Richard G. Poole, John W. Hasten,
Thomas B. White, William N. Bissell,
Michael N. Scott, Janet P. Kramer, Mark
L. Treon, Frank H. Hitch, Kenneth E.
Blankenship

**Neurogen Corporation Biomedical Research
Laboratory**
Branford, Connecticut, 1990, 1993, 1996,
1997, 1998
Client: Neurogen Corporation
Project Designer: William H. Grover
Project Team: James A. Coan (Phases I &
II), Roger U. Williams (Phases I, II, III,
IV, & V), E. Russell Learned (Phases III &
IV), Stephen B. Holmes (Phase II), Susan
L. Nelson (Phase V)

New Hearth Showroom
New York, New York, 1997
Client: D'Elia Associates
Project Designer: Mark Simon
Project Team: J. Richard Staub (project
manager), Todd E. Andrews, Sheryl A.
Milardo, Megan N. Gibson, Matthew C.
Conley

Norton Museum of Art
West Palm Beach, Florida, 1996, 1997
Client: Norton Museum of Art
Project Designers: Chad Floyd with Jean E.
Smajstrla
Project Team: Reno J. Migani, Jr. (job
captain), Jonathan G. Parks, Stephen B.
Holmes, Walker J. Burns III, Matthew C.
Conley, Roger U. Williams, Daniel H.
Glynn, Peter T. Coffin, Megan N. Gibson,
Sheryl A Milardo

Pall Corporation Technical Center
Port Washington, New York, 1995
Client: Pall Corporation
Project Designers: William H. Grover and
Dennis J. Dowd
Project Team: Walker J. Burns III, Steven E.
Tiezzi, Susan E. Wyeth, Daniel H. Glynn,
Roger U. Williams, C. Todd Delfosse,
Stephen B. Holmes, John M. Doyle,
Michael J. Milne, Jon M. Lavy, Sheryl A.
Milardo, Jamison Cox

Percarpio House
Guilford, Connecticut, 1979
Client: Brenda and Bernie Percarpio
Project Designer: Jefferson B. Riley

Pfizer Incorporated, Main Gate
Groton, Connecticut, 1994
Client: Pfizer U. S. Pharmaceuticals
Project Designers: Chad Floyd and James R.
Martin
Project Team: Robert L. Harper, Darin C.
Cook, Jonathan G. Parks, Steven E. Tiezzi,
Paul C. N. Mellblom

Pfizer Incorporated, South Gate
Groton, Connecticut, 1992
Client: Pfizer U. S. Pharmaceuticals
Project Designers: Chad Floyd and Jean E.
Smajstrla
Project Team: James R. Martin, George W.
Penniman, Darin C. Cook, Howard A.
Langner

Pfizer Incorporated, Technology Building
Groton, Connecticut, 1994
Client: Pfizer U. S. Pharmaceuticals
Project Designers: Chad Floyd and Nick
Deaver
Project Team: Stephen B. Holmes, Peter T.
Coffin, Edward J. Keagle, Michael J.
Milne, Sheri Bryant Lucero, James A.
Coan, Daniel H. Glynn, Darin C. Cook,
John M. Doyle, George W. Penniman,
Michelle R. LaFoe, James R. Martin,
Sheryl A. Milardo

Piazza d'Italia
New Orleans, Louisiana, 1975
Client: Office of the Mayor of New Orleans
Project Designers: Charles W. Moore
Associates with Urban Innovations Group
with August Perez Associates
Fountain Design: Charles W. Moore

**Pomfret School, Centennial Academic and Arts
Center**
Pomfret, Connecticut, 1995
Client: Pomfret School
Project Designers: Mark Simon and Nick
Deaver
Project Team: Peter T. Coffin, Mahdad
Saniee, Sheri Bryant Lucero, Paul L.
Shainberg, Darin C. Cook, Sheryl A.
Milardo, Charlotte C. Breed, Jonas M.
Goldberg, Robert L. Harper

Pond House
New England Island, 1992
Project Designers: Mark Simon and James
C. Childress
Project Team: Paul L. Shainberg, Stephen
B. Holmes, Kevin Henson, Leonard J.
Wyeth, Sheryl A. Milardo, Jonathan G.
Parks, Michael J. Crosbie, Robert
Coolidge, Michael J. Milne, Richard L.
King, Wanmaison Wanradzi, Paul C. N.
Mellblom

**PricewaterhouseCoopers Kwasha HR Solutions
Offices**
Fort Lee, New Jersey, 1996
Client: PricewaterhouseCoopers Kwasha HR
Solutions
Project Designers: Mark Simon and Jean E.
Smajstrla
Project Team: Peter T. Coffin, Edward J.
Keagle, Reno J. Migani, Jr., Darin C.
Cook, Daniel H. Glynn, Julia W. Harrison,
Peter A. Van Dusen, Jr., Jeffrey Gotta,
Sheryl A. Milardo, Christopher Arelt, Jon
M. Lavy, Walker J. Burns III, Megan N.
Gibson, Gregory E. Nucci, Mahdad
Saniee, David L. Huggins, Jonathan G.
Parks, Robert L. Harper, John M. Doyle,
Michael J. Crosbie, Michael Garner,
Stephen B. Holmes

Private Residence in Connecticut
Storm Ridge, Connecticut, 1986
Project Designer: William H. Grover
Project Team: Stephen L. Lloyd (project
manager), Walker J. Burns III

**Quinnipiac College, Carl Hansen Student
Center**
Hamden, Connecticut, 1991
Client: Quinnipiac College
Project Designers: Jefferson B. Riley with
Leonard J. Wyeth
Project Team: Ida Vorum (project manager,
Phase II); Jon M. Lavy, Robert G. Proctor,
Daniel H. Glynn, Michael J. Milne,
Michael J. Crosbie, Wanmaizan Wanradzi,
Paul L. Shainberg, Sheryl A. Milardo,
Margaret Wazuka

Quinnipiac College, Computer Center
Hamden, Connecticut, 1983
Client: Quinnipiac College
Project Designer: Jefferson B. Riley
Project Team: Leonard J. Wyeth (project
manager), Charles G. Mueller, Sheri
Bryant Lucero

Quinnipiac College, Dormitory
Hamden, Connecticut, 1983
Client: Quinnipiac College
Project Designer: Jefferson B. Riley
Project Team: Glenn W. Arbonies (project
manager), Leonard J. Wyeth

Quinnipiac College, Ledges Residence Hall
Hamden, Connecticut, 1998
Client: Quinnipiac College
Project Designers: Jefferson B. Riley with
Charles G. Mueller
Project Team: Mark Herter (job captain),
Michael V. LoSasso, John M. Doyle

**Quinnipiac College, Lender School of Business
Center**
Hamden, Connecticut, 1994
Client: Quinnipiac College
Project Designers: Jefferson B. Riley with
Leonard J. Wyeth
Project Team: Michael J. Milne, Robert G.
Proctor, Jon M. Lavy, James C. Childress,
John A. Simonetti, Wanmaizan Wanradzi,
Sheri Bryant Lucero, Michael J. Crosbie,
Jonathan G. Parks, George W. Penniman,
Christopher J. Payne, Michael
Garner, Paul L. Shainberg, Charlotte C.
Breed, Sheryl A. Milardo

Quinnipiac College, School of Law Center
Hamden, Connecticut, 1995
Client: Quinnipiac College
Project Designers: Jefferson B. Riley with
James C. Childress
Project Team: C. Todd Delfosse (job
captain), Ida Vorum, Michael Garner,
Daniel H. Glynn, John M. Doyle, Peter T.
Coffin, Christopher Arelt, J. Richard
Staub, Liam Winters, Charles G. Mueller,
Sheryl A. Milardo, Megan N. Gibson

Quinnipiac College, Suntraps
Hamden, Connecticut, 1984
Client: Quinnipiac College
Project Designer: Jefferson B. Riley
Project Team: J. Whitney Huber (project
manager), Leonard J. Wyeth

Reid House I
Cleveland Heights, Ohio, 1987
Client: Mr. and Mrs. James Reid
Project Designer: Jefferson B. Riley
Project Team: Walker J. Burns III (project
manager), Roger U. Williams, Jean E.
Smajstrla

Reid House II
Cape Cod, Massachusetts, 1991
Client: Mr. and Mrs. James Reid
Project Designer: Jefferson B. Riley
Project Team: Kyra Hauser and Jean E.
Smajstrla (project managers); Richard L.
King, Michael J. Crosbie, Ann Patterson,
Sheryl A. Milardo

Riley House I
Guilford, Connecticut, 1976, 1986
Client: Riley Family
Project Designer: Jefferson B. Riley

Riley House II
Guilford, Connecticut, 2000
Client: Jefferson B. Riley and
Karen Riley
Project Designers: Jefferson B. Riley and
Karen Riley

Riverdesign Springfield
Springfield, Massachusetts, 1981
Project Designer: Chad Floyd and Mark
Simon
Project Team: Jefferson B. Riley, Mark
Denton

Roanoke Design '79
Roanoke, Virginia, 1979
Client: City of Roanoke, Virginia
Project Designers: Chad Floyd and Charles
W. Moore (consulting)
Project Team: Leonard J. Wyeth (project
manager), Jefferson B. Riley, William H.
Grover, Robert L. Harper, Dean Ruth,
Glenn W. Arbonies
Associate Architect: Hayes, Seay, Mattern &
Mattern, Inc.

Roanoke Market Square
Roanoke, Virginia, 1985
Client: City of Roanoke, Virginia
Project Designer: Chad Floyd
Associate Architect: Hayes, Seay, Mattern &
Mattern, Inc.

Ross-Lacy House
Connecticut, 1989
Project Designers: Mark Simon and James
C. Childress
Project Team: Charles G. Mueller (job
captain)

Rowe House
Connecticut, 1981
Project Designer: William H. Grover
Project Team: Stephen L. Lloyd (project
manager)

Samuel's Clothing Store
Roanoke, Virginia, 1985
Client: Samuel's Clothing Store
Project Designer: Chad Floyd
Project Team: James R. Martin (project
manager), Sandy Scott

Shattuck House
Guilford, Connecticut, 1980
Client: Mr. and Mrs. James Shattuck
Project Designer: Jefferson B. Riley

Simon-Bellamy House I
Connecticut Shoreline, 1981
Client: Mark Simon and Penelope Bellamy
Project Designer: Mark Simon

Simon-Bellamy House II
Connecticut Shoreline, 1998
Client: Mark Simon and Penelope Bellamy
Project Designer: Mark Simon

Stepping Stones Museum for Children
Norwalk, Connecticut, 2000
Project Designers: Jefferson B. Riley with
Charles G. Mueller
Project Team: Michael V. LoSasso (project
manager), Mark Herter, Sheryl A.
Milardo, Jennifer Lewis, Michael R.
Stoddard, Susan Nelson, Andrew A.
Santaniello, Peggy V. Sullivan, Richard
Terrell, Peter A. Van Dusen, Jr., Jon M.
Lavy, Todd E. Andrews, Gregory E. Nucci,
Leslie McCombs, Stephen B. Holmes,
Jason Holtzman

Striar Jewish Community Center
Stoughton, Massachusetts, 1988
Client: South Area Jewish Community
Project Designer: Jefferson B. Riley
Project Team: Dennis J. Dowd (project
manager), J. Whitney Huber, Susan E.
Wyeth, Mahdad Saniee, Robert Coolidge,
Nick Deaver, Sheri Bryant Lucero,
Matthew C. Conley, Sheryl A. Milardo

Taplin House
Amesbury, Massachusetts, 1981
Client: Tom and Cindy Taplin
Project Designer: Jefferson B. Riley
Project Team: J. Whitney Huber (project
manager)

Thread City Crossing
Windham, Connecticut, 2000
Client: Connecticut Department of
Transportation
Project Designer: William H. Grover
Project Team: Walker J. Burns III (project
manager), Gregory E. Nucci
Bridge Engineers: Maguire Group
Connecticut, Inc.: Terry McCarthy,
Joseph Gonenc, Paul Ginotti, Shahvir
Vimadalal

Trudeau Institute
Saranac Lake, New York, 1999
Client: Trudeau Institute
Project Designer: James C. Childress and
Walker J. Burns III
Project Team: Sarah Weinkauf, Susan
Nelson, Sheryl A. Milardo, Megan N.
Gibson, Susan J. Pinckney, Lucy Ciletti,
Ted Tolis

**United Church of Christ Church House,
Amistad Chapel**
Cleveland, Ohio, 2000
Client: United Church of Christ
Project Designer: Jefferson B. Riley
Project Team: Michael V. LoSasso (project
manager), Sheryl A. Milardo, Catherine
Moore, Michael A. Sorano, Margaret A.
Molnar, Robert S. Oh, Christoper Nason
Consulting Architects: Valentine J. Schute,
Robert N. Wandel, Ann Vivian
Architect of Record: Planned
Environmental Design Corporation

United Church of Christ Church House, Hotel
Cleveland, Ohio, 2000
Client: United Church of Christ
Project Designer: Jefferson B. Riley
Project Team: Henry D. Altman (project
manager), Andrew A. Santaniello, Peter
A. Van Dusen, Jr., Leslie McCombs,
Jonathan G. Parks, Megan N. Gibson,
Nick Deaver, Padraic H. Ryan, J. Richard
Staub, Edward J. Keagle, Mark Verwoerdt,
James A. Russell

**University of Colorado, Health Sciences Center
Campus Center**
Denver, Colorado, 1986, Project
Client: University of Colorado
Project Designers: James C. Childress and
Mark Simon
Project Team: Nick Deaver (project
manager), Paul L. Shainberg, Padraic H.
Ryan, Jon M. Lavy
Architect of Record: Davis Partnership:
Hugh Brown (partner in charge), Brit
Probst (partner), Brian Erickson (project
manager), Lucy Ciletti, Steve Frye, J. D.
Nelson

University of Connecticut, Chemistry Building
Storrs, Connecticut, 1998
Client: University of Connecticut
Project Designer: Mark Simon
Project Team: James A. Coan (project
manager), Daniel H. Glynn (project
captain), C. Todd Delfosse, Jeffrey Gotta,
J. Richard Staub, Michael Garner, Sheryl
A. Milardo, Stephen B. Holmes, William
H. Grover, Jonathan G. Parks, Jonas M.
Goldberg, Michael R. Stoddard, Susan
Nelson

**University of Connecticut, Information Café,
Homer D. Babbidge Library**
Storrs, Connecticut, 1998
Client: University of Connecticut
Project Designers: Chad Floyd and Edward
J. Keagle
Project Team: Thomas J. Lodge (project
manager), Jennifer Lewis

**The University of Toledo, Honors Housing and
Academic Center**
Toledo, Ohio, 1993
Client: The University of Toledo
Project Designers: Chad Floyd and Nick
Deaver
Project Team: Michael Garner, Matthew C.
Conley, Charles G. Mueller, Robert G.
Proctor, Sheri Bryant Lucero, Sheryl A.
Milardo
Prime Architect: Seyfang Blanchard Duket
Porter: Robert F. Seyfang and Michael
Duket with Kevin J. Young

Watkins Glen Master Plan
Watkins Glen, New York, 1980
Client: Schuyler County Industrial
Development Agency
Project Designers: Chad Floyd and Charles
W. Moore (consulting)
Project Team: Mark Denton (project
manager), Frank Cheney, Jefferson B.
Riley, Cindy Hamilton, F. Bradford
Drake, James R. Martin, Stephen L. Lloyd

Watkins Glen Pier and Pavilion
Watkins Glen, New York, 1984
Client: Schuyler County Industrial
Development Agency
Project Designer: Chad Floyd
Project Team: F. Bradford Drake (project
manager), J. Whitney Huber

Watkins Glen "Timespell"
Watkins Glen State Park, Watkins Glen,
New York, 1982
Client: White River Development
Corporation
Project Designer: Chad Floyd
Project Team: J. Whitney Huber (project
manager)

Williams College Museum of Art
Williamstown, Massachusetts, 1986
Client: Trustees of Williams College
Project Designers: Robert L. Harper and
Charles W. Moore
Project Team: Richard L. King (project
manager, Phase I), Dennis J. Dowd
(project manager, Phase II), Charles G.
Mueller, Roger U. Williams, Susan E.
Wyeth, David Hajian, Walker J. Burns III,
Robert Coolidge, D. Randy Wilmot

Worcester Bridge
Worcester, Massachusetts, 1999
Client: Worcester Redevelopment Authority
and the City of Worcester
Project Designers: William H. Grover and
James C. Childress
Project Team: Padraic H. Ryan, Jonathan G.
Parks, Roger U. Williams, Michelle R.
Lafoe
Bridge Engineers: Maguire Group
Connecticut, Inc.: Richard Willett, Paul
Ginotti

Photographer and Delineator Credits

Photography Credits

Alinari/Art Resource, NY: 72 (3)

Peter Aaron/Esto: 90 (11); 127 (6)

Morley Baer: 40 (9)

Bruno Barbey/Magnum Photos: 98 (1)

The Beinecke Rare Book and Manuscript Library, Yale University: 103 (10)

Robert Benson: 10; 58 (22); 131 (17); 160 (74); 246 (4); 248 (20,21)

Melinda Blauvelt: 100 (4,5); 102 (7,9); 103 (11); 104 (13); 106 (16); 181 (132)

Antoine Bootz: 200 (15)

Steven Brooke: 201 (18)

Steve Carter: 128 (7); 212 (2)

Centerbrook Architects: 34 (1); 35 (3); 58 (20); 62 (1); 132 (2); 133 (4); 181 (133); 192 (1); 227 (15); 246 (1–3,5,7); 247 (8–11); 248 (14–19); 249 (22–27)

Langdon Clay: 75 (8)

Michael Cooper: 50 (3)

Corbis/Bettmann: 34 (2)

Corbis/Ric Ergenbright: 99 (2)

Corbis/Robert Holmes: 102 (8)

Michael J. Crosby: 142 (20)

Dartmouth College: 184 (2,3)

Mark Denton: 166 (85)

Joanne Devereux: 55 (12)

John Morris Dixon: 232 (6)

Chad Floyd of Centerbrook: 52 (5); 104 (12); 105 (14,15); 107 (18); 108 (20); 111 (28); 161 (76); 170 (103); 175 (113); 184 (1); 185 (4); 212 (1)

Scott Frances: 235 (11)

Scott Frances/Esto: 24 (1); 222 (4); 232 (7)

Jeff Goldberg/Esto: 13 (4); 16 (8,9); 17 (10); 19 (17); 20 (18,19); 21 (20); 26 (7); 27; 28 (10); 29 (11); 31 (15); 32 (17,18); 33; 45 (14–16); 52 (7); 53 (8); 55 (11); 56 (14,16); 58 (19); 60 (25,26); 61; 67 (21,22); 68 (24); 69 (25,26); 78 (13–15); 79 (16); 80 (18,19); 81 (20,21); 82 (22,23); 83 (24,26); 87 (3); 88 (6); 92 (16); 93 (18,21); 94 (22); 96 (28); 122 (5); 123: 127 (4,5); 129 (11,12); 136 (6); 140 (14); 144 (25,26); 151 (47); 160 (72,73); 164 (82);165 (84); 167 (92); 170 (102); 175 (116); 176 (121); 178 (125); 179 (127–129); 182 (135); 187 (6,7); 188 (9); 190 (11); 191 (12,13); 192 (2,3); 194 (4); 195 (5,6); 197; 198 (12); 199 (14); 200 (16); 201 (17); 203 (2,3); 204 (4,5); 205 (6,7); 206 (8); 208 (18,19); 209 (20–22); 226 (11–13); 227 (14); 228 (17,18); 229 (19); 233 (9); 236 (14,15); 237 (17); 238 (18); 239 (21); 240 (4); 241 (6,7); 244 (1,2); 245 (3–5)

William H. Grover: 12 (1); 13 (3); 118 (2–5); 119 (6,7); 132 (1,3); 210 (1,2); 240 (1,3); 241 (15)

Mick Hales: 57 (17,18)

George Heinrich: 39 (7); 161 (77)

Lizzie Himmel: 148 (39)

Brenda Huffman: 100 (3); 172 (106)

Timothy Hursley: 26 (5); 28 (9); 35 (4); 36 (1); 37 (2); 59 (24); 64 (16); 73 (4); 75 (7); 84 (27); 92 (17); 157 (64,66); 195 (7); 196 (9); 202 (1); 223 (6); 230 (1); 232 (4); 234 (10); 247 (12,13)

Timm Jamieson: 107 (19); 109 (23,24)

Shin Koyama: 52 (6)

Laurie Kress: 140 (13); 145 (27); 147 (35); 148 (37); 149 (41); 152 (48); 153 (50); 154 (53); 156 (60,62); 158 (67); 167 (90); 170 (101,104); 179 (126)

Chris Little: 167 (91)

Steven L. Lloyd: 144 (24)

Lorenz and Williams: 110 (25,26)

Sven Martson: 46 (18)

Peter Mauss/Esto: 14 (5); 15 (7); 38 (3,4); 91 (12,13); 94 (24); 95 (25); 142 (21); 148 (40); 152 (49); 161 (75); 169 (97,98)

Norman McGrath: 22 (21–23); 23 (24); 25 (2,4); 29 (12); 30 (13,14); 31 (16); 46 (17); 55 (13); 58 (21); 59 (23); 70 (1); 71; 76 (10,11); 77 (12); 85 (28–30); 89 (9); 97 (30); 126 (2,3); 128 (9); 130 (15); 134 (2); 135; 137 (8); 138 (10); 145 (30); 146 (32); 147 (33,36); 150 (46); 154 (52,54,55); 155 (57,58); 156 (59,61); 166 (86–88); 167 (89); 168 (95); 175 (115); 183 (136); 196 (8); 210 (4); 232 (8); 236 (12,13)

Brian McNally: 19 (15,16)

Museum of Modern Art Film Stills Archive: 54 (9)

Museum of Modern Art, New York: 231 (2): Sörenson-Popitz, Irmgard, Suspended Construction, 1924. 231 (3): Rietveld, Gerrit. Highbacked Chair, 1919. Steamed beechwood, laquered terminals, 36 11/16 x 23 1/16 x 18". Manufacturer: Cassina, S.p.A., Milan, Italy. Gift of the manufacturer.

Nebraska State Historical Society: 12 (2)

Robert Perron: 246 (6)

Reuters/Corbis-Bettman/Gary Hershorn: 101 (6)

Jefferson B. Riley of Centerbrook: 86 (1); 87 (4); 89 (7); 90 (10); 92 (15); 93 (20); 97 (29); 129 (10); 134 (1); 136 (4,5); 138 (9); 139 (11,12); 143 (22); 148 (38); 150 (43,45); 155 (56); 157 (63,65); 159 (69); 160 (71); 163 (79); 164 (81); 165 (83); 168 (93,94); 169 (99,100); 173 (108); 174 (110,111); 175 (114,117); 176 (118); 177 (122); 180 (130); 182 (134); 240 (2)

Kevin Roche John Dinkeloo and Associates: 222 (5)

Steve Rosenthal: 44 (13); 54 (10); 56 (15); 145 (29); 163 (80); 173 (109): 186 (5); 189 (10); 199 (13); 237 (16); 238 (19,20)

Guido Alberto Rossi/The Image Bank, 2000: 178 (124)

Shelburne Museum, Shelburne, Vermont, Mark Sashara: 232 (5)

Jackson Smith: 40 (10)

Timespell: 111 (27)

Brian Vanden Brink: 46 (19); 47 (20,21); 149 (42); 150 (44); 158 (68); 159 (70)

Paul Warchol: 39 (6,8); 86 (2); 141 (18); 162; 168 (96); 171 (105); 172 (107); 174 (112); 180 (131); 183 (137)

Judith Watts: 153 (51)

Marion Wesp: 118 (1)

WDBJ-TV, Roanoke: 214 (6,7); 218 (13,14); 219 (15)

Nick Wheeler: 41 (11); 42–43; 124 (7); 125 (8); 126 (1); 141 (16); 196 (10)

Woodruff/Brown: 227 (16)

WOET-TV, Dayton: 128 (8); 212 (3); 213 (4); 214 (5)

WSYE-TV, Watkins Glen: 215 (8): 216 (10,11); 217 (12)

WWLP-TV, Springfield: 215 (9)

Yale Dramatic Association: 48 (1); 49 (2)

Delineator Credits

John Blood and William H. Grover of Centerbrook (watercolorist); 188 (8)

Centerbrook Architects: 63 (6,8,10,12,14)

Centerbrook Architects and Jill Childress (watercolorist): 65 (18); 66 (19); 120 (1); 121 (3,4); 220 (2); 224 (8)

Centerbrook Architects with Chris Dunn and Mark Hamelin: 224 (7)

James C. Childress of Centerbrook: 62 (2–5); 130 (14)

Nick Deaver: 207 (9–15)

Nick Deaver and Jill Childress (watercolorist): 66 (20); 221 (3)

Jeffrey Gotta of Centerbrook: 210 (3)

William H. Grover of Centerbrook: 112 (1–4); 113 (5,6); 114 (7); 115 (8); 116 (9); 117; 131 (16)

Eugene Lee: 51 (4)

Reno J. Migani, Jr. and William H. Grover (watercolorist) of Centerbrook: 207 (16)

Mark Simon, Nick Deaver and James C. Childress of Centerbrook: 63 (7,9,11,13,15)

Edith Spencer: 25 (3)

Sarah E. Weinkauf of Centerbrook: 65 (17)

Model Credits

Lucy M. Ciletti of Centerbrook: 225 (9,10)

Laura Martin of Centerbrook: 130 (13)